create your own
hand-printed cloth

STAMP, SCREEN & STENCIL WITH EVERYDAY OBJECTS

RAYNA GILLMAN

C&T PUBLISHING

Text copyright © 2008 by Rayna Gillman

Artwork copyright © 2008 by C&T Publishing, Inc.

Publisher: Amy Marson

Creative Director: Gailen Runge

Acquisitions Editor: Jan Grigsby

Editor: Lynn Koolish

Technical Editors: Elin Thomas and Gailen Runge

Copyeditor/Proofreader: Wordfirm Inc.

Design Director/Cover & Book Designer: Christina D. Jarumay

Production Coordinator: Kirstie L. Pettersen

Photography by Luke Mulks and Diane Pedersen of C&T Publishing unless otherwise noted

Published by C&T Publishing, Inc., P.O. Box 1456, Lafayette, CA 94549

Library of Congress Cataloging-in-Publication Data

Gillman, Rayna,

  Create your own hand-printed cloth : stamp, screen & stencil with everyday objects / Rayna Gillman.

     p. cm.

  Summary: "Create original cloth for quilts or wearable art by printing with found or recycled objects from around the house or hardware store, using a variety of pigments and surface design techniques including screen printing, stamping, rubbings, monoprinting with a gelatin plate, and working with soy wax for easy batik"--Provided by publisher.

  Includes index.

  ISBN 978-1-57120-439-4 (paper trade : alk. paper)

  1. Textile printing. 2. Dyes and dyeing, Domestic. I. Title.

  TT852.G55 2008

  667'.38--dc22

                                          2007038300

Printed in China

10 9 8 7 6 5 4 3 2

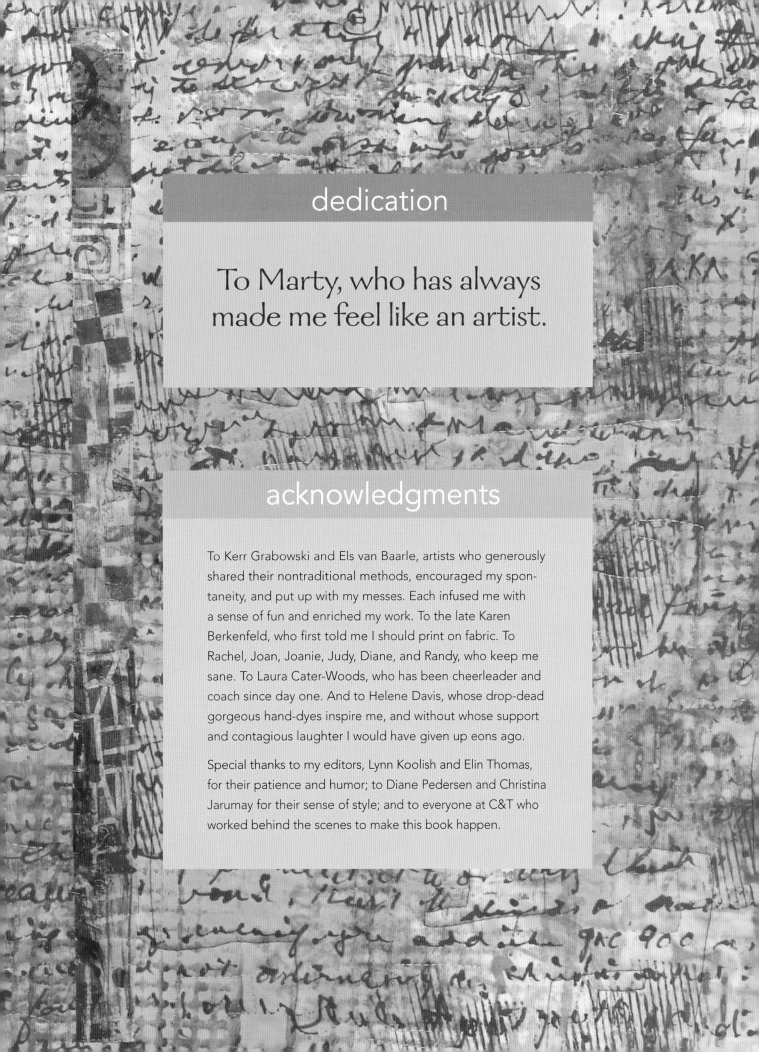

dedication

To Marty, who has always
made me feel like an artist.

acknowledgments

To Kerr Grabowski and Els van Baarle, artists who generously
shared their nontraditional methods, encouraged my spontaneity, and put up with my messes. Each infused me with
a sense of fun and enriched my work. To the late Karen
Berkenfeld, who first told me I should print on fabric. To
Rachel, Joan, Joanie, Judy, Diane, and Randy, who keep me
sane. To Laura Cater-Woods, who has been cheerleader and
coach since day one. And to Helene Davis, whose drop-dead
gorgeous hand-dyes inspire me, and without whose support
and contagious laughter I would have given up eons ago.

Special thanks to my editors, Lynn Koolish and Elin Thomas,
for their patience and humor; to Diane Pedersen and Christina
Jarumay for their sense of style; and to everyone at C&T who
worked behind the scenes to make this book happen.

contents

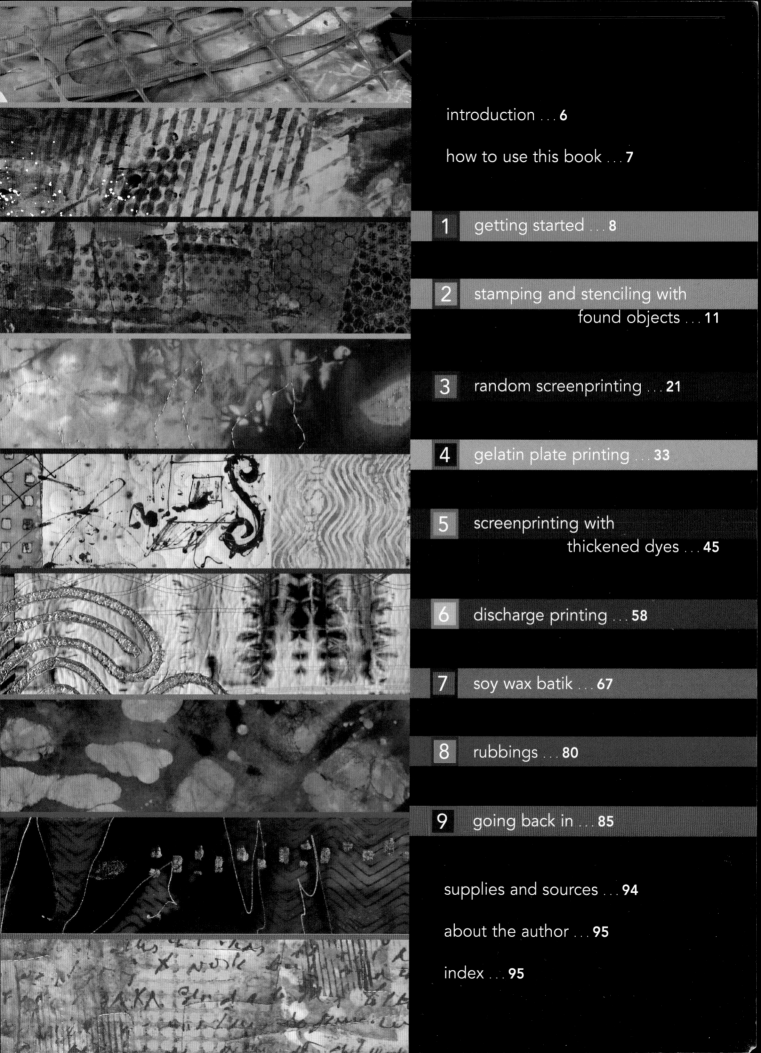

introduction

Every time I teach a surface design workshop, whether it is Printing with Found Objects or Printing from Your Pantry (also known as gelatin plate monoprinting), the enthusiasm that bubbles in the room tells me that my way of working strikes a chord. Because most workshops are time-limited, there's rarely the opportunity to try it all. I've had so many requests for follow-up information that my class notes have evolved into what you are reading.

For many of us, the words "surface design" can be a bit intimidating. They were for me until I realized that anything you do to change fabric is surface design—grab a brush and make lines, apply paint with a rubber stamp, remove the color from the fabric—all instant surface design! It doesn't need to be complicated or expensive, and it doesn't have to take forever. You can make any fabric your own in no time flat, and have a wonderful time doing it.

For me, surface design started as an experiment and became an obsession. I was in an on-campus summer quilting workshop and didn't have quite the right commercial fabric for the piece I was making. On a whim, I borrowed some paint, a brush, and a rubber stamp, and went to work. The resulting fabric wasn't gorgeous but it was just what I needed, and I was hooked. The found-objects light went on as I spotted grids of orange construction fence around the campus and envisioned the design possibilities. That night, armed with scissors, I "found" a bit of fence, and the rest is history. Every time I saw fencing made of plastic mesh that was a different shape or size, I begged the construction guys for "just a six-inch piece." They always asked, "Whaddya need it for?" And my answer was, "I'm an artist."

Excited by other design prospects, I haunted Home Depot, house-wares departments, dollar stores, and garage sales. I bought a single ceramic tile, six assorted drawer pulls, and metal grids of every size and shape. My kitchen counter became a repository of mesh onion bags, Styrofoam trays, and cut-up takeout container lids. My habitually neat husband constantly asked, "Is this here for a reason?" But I knew he finally got it when, after several years, he brought home a plastic candy box liner and asked, "Can you use this?"

how to use this book

- If you've taken a workshop from me, this book will serve as an illustrated reminder of what you did and a handbook for trying things we didn't have time to do.

- If the phrase "surface design" has mystified you but you've wanted to try it, this informal approach to printing on fabric will get you started.

- If you are an experienced surface designer, I'm betting you will find one or more new approaches, variations, or materials to experiment with.

- For all of you, I hope this book will be a comprehensive resource and jumping-off point for your own improvisations and imagination. These techniques are low cost, low tech, low key, and high impact!

My basic principles here and in the classroom are simple:

- Work quickly. Don't overanalyze. Be spontaneous and see where this spontaneity leads you.

- Don't worry about being neat. You can buy neat in a store.

- Experiment! Ask yourself, "What if I did it this way?" and then try it.

- It's okay if you don't like it. You will, next week. And if you don't, you have several options:

  –Someone else might like it, and you can trade.

  –You can add another layer or two.

  –You can cut it up.

- Relax and have fun while you're playing.

getting started

CHAPTER 1

found objects

Anything is fair game for printing if it has texture, bumps, holes, or an interesting shape. Okay, I admit it: *found* can be a bit of a stretch. You can find things when you're out for a walk, going through your junk drawer, or putting out the recycling. These are free.

After a while, people will start giving you things—also free. If you don't mind paying for them, you can find plenty of items at the hardware store, in the supermarket kitchenware aisle, at the dollar store, or at garage sales. Once you start to look at everything differently there is no end to what you can find. The list is endless, but here are a few places to look:

- Kitchen drawers
- Office
- Hardware or housewares store
- Yard
- Street
- Toy department

The following are some of the items that are good for stamping, rubbing, screening, and monoprinting. Once you start looking at things as printing tools, you will come up with lots of other ideas.

- Plastic, rubber, or metal objects with holes or bumps
- Sponges
- Bubble wrap

- Corks
- Drawer pulls
- Textured foam meat trays
- Plastic berry baskets
- Corrugated cardboard (This works well for stamping. It is disposable, but if you want to use it a number of times you may want to put a coat of gel medium on it to keep it waterproof for an extended period.)

Household items

Kitchen hot pads

Found objects for printing

fabric for printing

Any tightly woven natural-fiber fabric will work with any of the techniques in this book.

- Cotton
- Light- to medium-colored commercial fabrics that read as solids
- Hand-dyes
- Unbleached muslin
- Dark-colored commercial fabrics or hand-dyes for discharge
- Silk
- Rayon
- Linen

NOTE: PFD (prepared for dyeing) cottons work best with dyes. If you can't get PFD fabrics (see Supplies and Sources on page 94), wash your fabric to remove any finishes. I prefer to use Synthrapol and hot water, but other people have had success using hot water and liquid detergents with no additives, fragrances, or brighteners.

paints and dyes for printing

PAINTS

Water-based textile paints or screening inks for fabric are best. Fabric or textile paints come in a variety of consistencies and brands. Some are thicker, such as ProChem's ProFab paints. Other brands can be thinner. Each gives slightly different results and all become permanent by heat setting with an iron for 3–5 minutes.

What about acrylics? You may already have some acrylic paints in your studio, especially if you have worked on canvas. Acrylics work well for gelatin plate printing, but acrylic paints will change the hand or feel of your fabric and can leave a plastic-like surface on your textiles. If you are making an art piece to hang on the wall, this may not matter. But if you are making garments or quilts to use, you are better off with textile paints.

If you want to use acrylics you have on hand, you can add fabric medium or silkscreen medium. Or, you can do what I have done in a pinch: rinse out the fabric before you heat set it. Some of the color will come off, but so will the plasticky surface of the paint. I have done this many times if the color I need is acrylic.

One more word about acrylic paints if you are using screens: they dry very quickly and can clog your screen's pores unless you wash the paint out immediately. To keep paint from clogging the screen, wash it as soon as you have finished using it. If you want to reuse it immediately, dry it with a paper towel or, even better, a hair dryer. Some paint may stain the screen; this is not significant. If you can see through the mesh, it is not clogged.

DYES

I use Procion MX fiber-reactive dyes. Soda ash or dye activator is used to set or activate the dyes. Sodium alginate is used to thicken dyes. If you have never worked with dyes, this is a good way to start; thickened dyes are easy to handle, won't spill, and will enable you to get different effects than you get with paints. See pages 45–47 for instructions on thickening dyes.

Paints and dyes

DISCHARGE AGENTS

You may want to take the color out of fabric as well as putting it in. We'll take a look at the different methods and substances for removing color; bleach products and other products will give you varied results. See pages 58–66 for discharge techniques.

resists

A resist blocks out the paint, dye, or other pigment you are using so the area of the fabric where you've put the resist will remain unprinted. There are many types of resists.

FOUND-OBJECT RESISTS

Everyday objects such as mesh onion bags, sink mats, corrugated cardboard, and any flat objects with texture, bumps, or holes can be used as resists. You can get myriad effects, depending on how you use these objects. Possibilities include the following:

- Using a resist on top of fabric under a screen
- Using the imprint of a resist that remains on a screen
- Using the paint left on a resist as a stamp

PAPER RESISTS

Newspapers, paper towels, freezer paper—you can probably find all of these in your kitchen. We get two daily and three weekly newspapers; most go into the recycling bin, but to me they are art supplies! Tear them or cut them—they all give slightly different results.

OTHER RESISTS

Blue school glue gel and soy wax are easy-to-remove substances you may want to experiment with. Both are inexpensive and nontoxic.

work surfaces

While a hard surface works better if you are stamping with a soft stamp, in most cases you will want to work on a padded surface. You can use pink foam insulation board covered with a 1/2″ layer of foam rubber, a plastic drop cloth, and an old sheet. This is what covers my worktable.

However, I have recently added a 1/2″-thick pad of felt carpet padding to protect the plastic from damage by hot wax or an iron. You can simply cover a table with two layers of felt or felt carpet padding.

Carpet padding

If space is at a premium, you can make a 24″ × 24″ (or larger) lightweight, portable print surface by cutting foam insulation board and foam rubber to size, covering the rubber with plastic, and duct taping or stapling it to the underside of the board. Cover the plastic with an old sheet. If you need a hard surface, you can lay a sheet of Plexiglas or fiberboard on top. Or, if you are doing batik, add a layer of felt carpet padding.

other supplies and equipment

Depending on the techniques you want to use, you may also need the following:

- Screens and squeegees for screenprinting
- Duct tape
- Masking tape
- Aluminum foil pans
- Unflavored gelatin
- Measuring cup and plastic spoons
- Plastic containers
- Spray bottle with water
- Iron
- Hair dryer
- Newspaper
- Rubber brayers
- Foam brushes

We'll cover all these subjects later in more detail, so let's get started!

stamping and stenciling with found objects

junk-drawer printing

Chances are you have a number of rubber stamps in your studio that you have either bought or carved. So do I; they are indispensable for adding special touches to almost any fabric. But you also have a treasure trove of potential stamps in your kitchen, garage, or basement that will give your fabric individuality that can't be bought. Hardware stores, thrift stores, and yard sales are also great sources for stamping implements.

You can use almost anything as a stamp: forks, wire whisks, corrugated cardboard, drawer pulls, even foam pool noodles sliced crosswise. No matter how ordinary your found objects are, you can use them to print extraordinary fabric.

Just to give you some ideas, Marni Goldshlag printed the green base fabric with a sink mat, a rubber pad with a chevron pattern, and a metal grid that covers gutters so the leaves won't fall in. The gold squares were painted through the holes of the sink mat.

Fabric printed with corrugated cardboard, sequin waste, and snow fence

Sunlight on the River, Marni Goldshlag, 23½″ × 23½″

The circles are stamped with lids from take out containers.

Check those junk drawers—once you start to look you'll see everything with new eyes.

supplies

- Scissors
- 1″ foam brushes
- Foam roller
- Foam tray
- Plastic spoons
- Two rubber brayers
- Spray bottle for water
- Assorted colors of water-based fabric paints
- Assorted household objects such as bubble wrap, sponges, drawer pulls, sink mats, and so on

preparation

Place your washed and ironed fabric on a padded surface (see instructions for making a padded surface on page 10), and pin every 2″–3″ around the edges. This will keep the fabric nicely stretched. All it takes is a "what if?" point of view and willingness to experiment. Don't forget: if you don't like the first layer, you can always add another one.

found-object stamps

Any material that has a raised repeat design, such as bubble wrap or corrugated cardboard, makes an ideal stamp. For example, to use bubble wrap, follow these steps:

1. Spoon paint onto a foam tray, and use a sponge brush or brayer to cover the surface of the bubble wrap with paint.

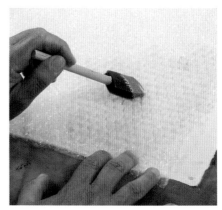
Apply paint to bubble wrap.

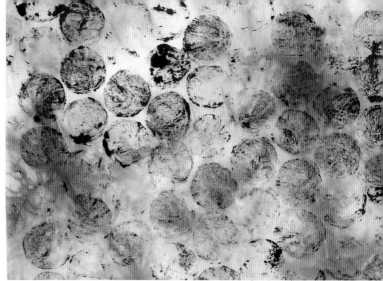

2. Place the painted bubble wrap face down on the fabric, and roll a brayer gently over it, or, even better, lay the bubble wrap on the face-up fabric, and use your hands to smooth it down. This method will keep the bubbles from bursting and will enable you to reuse it for more printing.

Another fabric printed using bubble wrap

Place painted bubble wrap over fabric, and smooth with your hands.

 If the printed fabric will be used as a background, apply paint sparingly so it does not overwhelm subsequent layers.

Paint another piece of bubble wrap, and roll with a brayer.

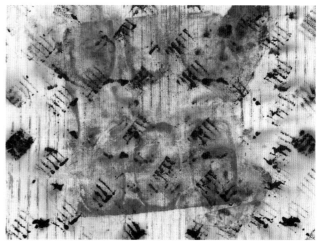

Fabric printed with corrugated cardboard strips

The design created by bubble wrap

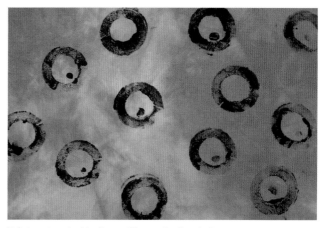

Fabric printed with slices of foam pipe insulation

 You will need two brayers: one for rolling paint onto the stamp and a clean one for printing.

found-object stencils

In the piece below, Jeanne Surber used recycled cardboard packing material and a piece of scrap plastic with holes in it for stenciling. She also used a decorative tile, rubber stamp, and clothespin for stamping.

Plastic snow fence used as a stencil

 tip *When you use paint sparingly, you will see the roller's texture.*

The cut-apart sides and bottoms of green plastic berry baskets make great stencils, as do any items with holes or openings.

Yin & Yang, Jeanne Surber, 14¾″ × 18¼″

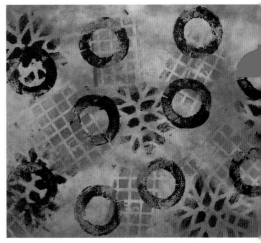

Fabric printed with berry basket stencils and foam insulation stamps

Experiment by using only one item for both stamping and stenciling on the same piece of cloth.

As you work, you will discover that some items are better for stamping and others work better as stencils. Flat items with holes or openings that will rest directly on the fabric usually work well as stencils. Foam rollers and brayers work particularly well for applying paint.

Plastic grid used for stenciling

Plastic grid used for stamping

You can also place the grid over the lines you've already stamped and then roll paint through the spaces, for a two-color print.

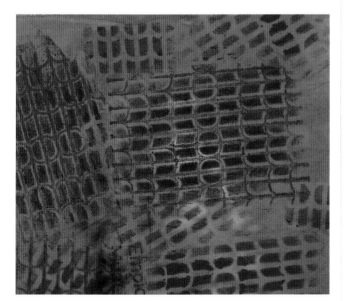

Stenciling over printed fabric

Liz Berg created the fabric for the quilt below by stamping and stenciling with a variety of textured items.

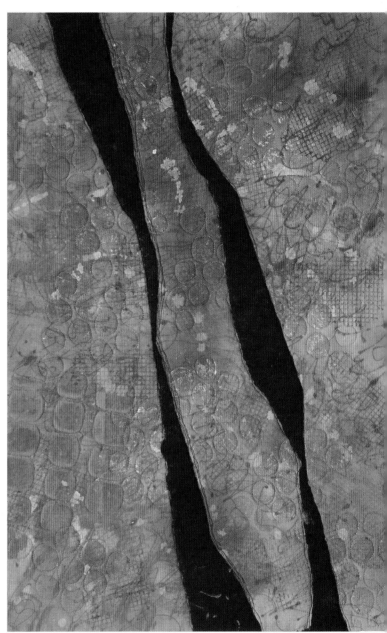

Split, Liz Berg, 19″ × 28″

printing dry or wet

You can print on dry fabric or damp fabric. You may also want to print on dry cloth and spritz it with water afterward to spread the paint a bit; the results will be different each time. What determines whether you print on damp fabric or on dry fabric? It can be your mood, the effect you want, or just impulse. Every time you print, it's an experiment.

PRINTING ON DRY FABRIC

Even simple objects, such as this foam insulation block, can give your fabric texture, and when you are printing on dry fabric, the texture will vary depending on whether you use a foam brush or a brayer to apply the paint.

Dry fabric printed using foam block; paint applied with foam brush

Dry fabric printed using foam block; paint applied with brayer

PRINTING ON WET FABRIC

When the fabric is damp it will absorb more paint and the lines will be softer.

Wet fabric printed using foam block; paint applied with foam brush

Wet fabric printed using foam block; paint applied with brayer

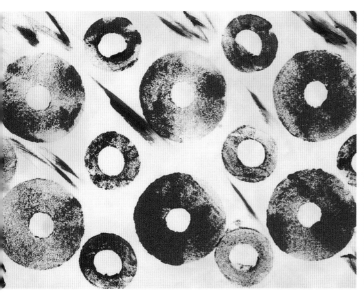

Dry fabric printed with slices of foam noodles

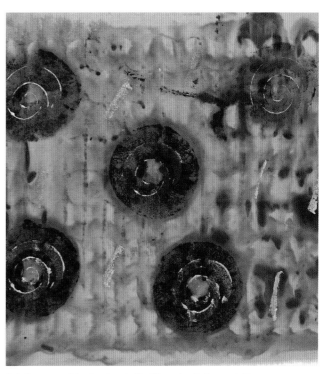

Fabric sprayed (not saturated) with water *before* printing

You can see how much crisper the dry prints are, although the same stamps printed the wet and the dry fabrics. Try printing several ways to see what works for you.

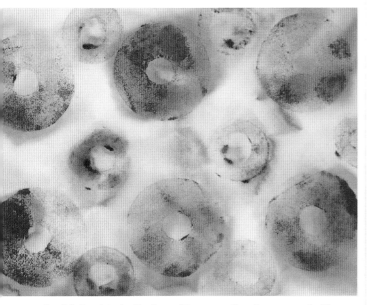

Dry fabric printed with slices of foam noodles, then sprayed with water for watercolor effect

two-for-one printing

What happens when an item you'd like to stamp with doesn't hold the paint well? Some smooth or shiny plastics with narrow surfaces fall into this category. These items will need a bit more pressure than objects that are not as slick, so you will need to use two brayers. And that's where the bonus comes in.

FIRST PRINT

1. Spoon paint onto a palette, and cover a roller evenly with a generous amount of paint.

2. Roll the paint onto the grid.

Paint applied to grid

3. Lay the paint-covered brayer aside, *roller side up* (this is important).

4. Place the grid on the fabric, paint side down, and go over it with a clean, dry brayer. The resulting imprint will be an outline because the paint doesn't adhere completely to the grid.

Clean brayer used on grid

Lift the object to reveal the design. Note: The paint doesn't adhere to the entire surface; the imprint is an outline.

BONUS PRINT

Now for the bonus!

1. Pick up the brayer you put aside after you applied paint to the grid.

Brayer with paint from grid

2. Roll the brayer across another area of the cloth, and watch something surreal unfold.

Print from brayer

This is an imprint you can't get with any other method. The roller has picked up the imprint from the grid but distorts the image because the brayer is round. Below, you can see the stamped image on the top left of the fabric, along with the variations made by what is left on the brayer.

For me, this imprint is the best part because it is a surprise—unforeseen, unpredictable, and unrepeatable. My students call it two-for-one printing.

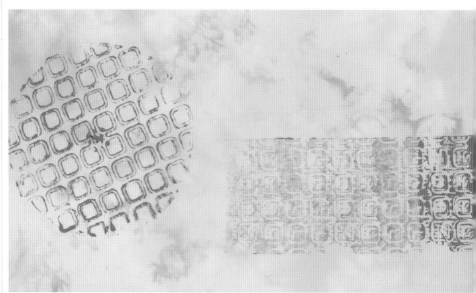

Two-for-one printing

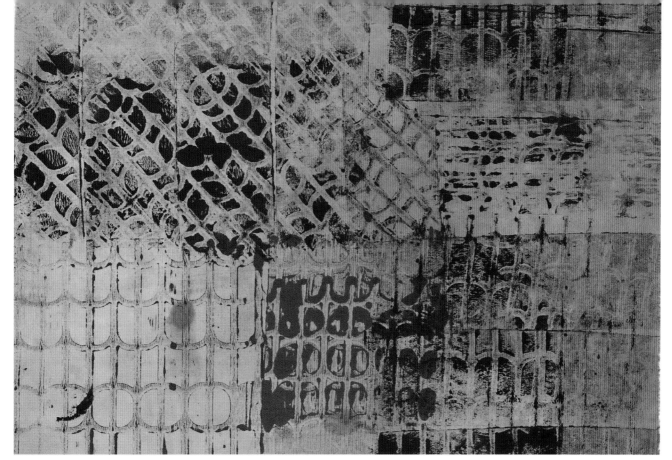

This is another example of two-for-one printing.

knowing when enough is enough

Once you get into the swing of things, it's hard to stop. Your fabric looks better and better as you keep adding and adding...until you realize you should have stopped earlier. Oops, you've got mud. This piece has so much printing on it that it is useful only when it is cut into small pieces.

Too much! This is useful only when cut into small pieces.

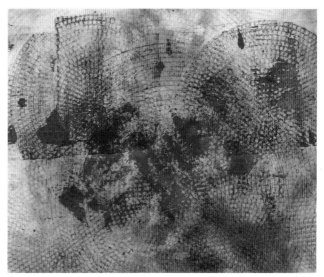

No discernable pattern; good background fabric

My advice (which I don't always follow) is this: If you have to ask yourself whether it needs one more dab, the answer is probably "no." Stop, put the fabric aside, and look at it the next day. Chances are it's just right. And if it isn't, you've had the benefit of a night's sleep and some perspective.

In the quilt below, the added yellow is exactly what the fabric needs to make a strong visual statement.

Lumière, Anne Harmon Datko, 16″ × 26″

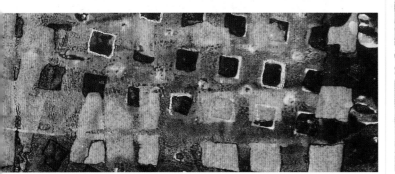

If you really don't like what you've printed or feel the paint is too thick or too dark, wash it out. *Yes, wash it out.* Before you iron the fabric to heat set it, run it under warm water, and let the paint flow down the drain. A waste of paint? Maybe, but it's worth it. Some of the paint will remain in the fabric, but it will be almost like a shadow—a transparent first layer that you can overprint to create a more complex piece.

The gray rectangles in the piece below were printed with black paint but were too dark for my taste. I ran the cloth under the faucet and the rectangles became much lighter. Eventually, I added layers and it became a wholecloth quilt.

Solstice (detail), Rayna Gillman (full quilt on page 25)

There is help for almost everything, as you will see in Going Back In, starting on page 85.

random screenprinting

For many of us, screenprinting is both intriguing and intimidating. So many people have said, "I've always wanted to work with screens but never knew where to start." In the context of this book, screenprinting is not complicated. It doesn't require any real planning, which is why I call it random screenprinting. In most cases, you will work spontaneously—and use the results as a springboard for your creativity.

So if you are aiming for perfection every time (or at all), my way of screenprinting might not be for you. There are many variables when you screen: the consistency and amount of paint or thickened dye, the amount of pressure and the angle of the squeegee, and the resist or stencil material. You'll never get the same result twice—and with my techniques, you don't want to. Enjoy the freedom you will have to take advantage of the unexpected, to find your own way of working, and to discover your own sense of design.

Red Zone, Rayna Gillman, 25″ x 24½″

supplies

- Textile screening inks
- 1 or more silkscreens (see next page)
- Masking tape
- Blue school glue gel
- Newspaper
- Wire or plastic grids or flat items with holes, such as sequin waste or plastic fence
- Freezer paper
- Brayer
- Squeegees (see next page)

SILKSCREENS

You can purchase screens inexpensively from art supply stores, or you can make your own. I've done both and opt for the purchased ones. If you want to make your own, information is available in libraries or on the Internet. Otherwise, I recommend starting with a 10″ × 12″ screen in either 8xx, 10xx, or 12xx mesh. The 8xx has a more open weave and is easier to clean than the 12xx. The more tightly woven 12xx gives more detail, but for the techniques we are using in this book you don't need to worry about detail, so any of these sizes will do. Scrub your new screen with detergent and a brush, rinse it, and let it dry. If you protect the wood frame with a coat or two of polyurethane, it will last longer than if you leave the wood raw. Or, you may want to cover the wood frame with duct tape to protect it. In any case, you will want to lay a strip of duct tape across the screen at one end to act as a well in which to put your paint. If you're like me, you'll want to start with at least three screens: one for paint, one for dye, and one for good measure.

SQUEEGEES

Don't buy a traditional wood and rubber squeegee; it will be too big and heavy for this kind of screenprinting. Your best bet is to use alternative squeegees such as plastic wallpaper smoothers from the paint store or, my favorite, plastic auto paint scrapers that come in different sizes up to 6″. In a pinch, you can't beat the flexibility of an expired credit card.

Screening supplies

preparation

Wash and iron your fabric, and pin it to a padded surface (see page 10 for preparing a printing surface), stretched as tautly as possible. This will prevent wrinkles and keep the fabric from coming up when you pull the screen away after you print.

screenprinting with stencils

The best resists for random screenprinting are inexpensive, disposable, and likely to be in your kitchen drawers.

MASKING-TAPE STENCILS

Masking tape or painter's tape makes simple resists that will yield abstract, sophisticated results, even if you have never screened before. The tape will stay on the screen until you remove it, so you can use it numerous times.

1. Tear or cut strips of masking tape, and apply them to the back (the flat side) of a blank screen.

Apply masking-tape strips to the screen.

2. Place the screen on the fabric, tape side down. Spoon the paint into the well along one side of the screen.

Place the screen on the fabric, and spoon paint into the well.

3. Hold the squeegee at a 45° angle, and pull the paint toward you.

Pull the paint toward you with a squeegee.

Not enough paint to cover the screen? Don't worry—just spoon on some more paint, and spread it with the squeegee. Since this is random screenprinting, you can work in all directions across the screen until it is covered.

Add paint, and use a squeegee until the screen surface is covered.

 tip *Pigments will stain the screen but will not affect the results. After you wash out the screen with detergent and hot water, hold it up to the light. If you can see through the mesh, the screen is not clogged.*

4. Carefully lift the screen from the fabric and admire your work.

Lift the screen.

You can make your taped designs as simple or complex as you wish, although simple can be very dramatic.

This screened design was created with tape.

Judy Rys used jagged edges of torn tape to create a strong visual effect that combines well with other hand-printed and commercial fabrics.

Branching Out, Judy Rys, 17½″ × 19″

NEWSPAPER STENCILS

Newspapers make good temporary stencils that are easy to print with. You can tape them to the screen, but I find it easier to just place them on the fabric. The first time you screen over them, they are likely to adhere to the screen. And if they don't, that's okay too. In fact, after you have screened with them several times, they may stick to the fabric. This can present other design possibilities, as I discovered.

The first time I screenprinted, I tore random shapes and strips out of newspaper. After a while, some of them adhered to the paint on the fabric and I left them there as collage. After the paint and paper had dried, I saw unexpected images in the fabric and went back in with colored pencils and other collage elements to enhance them.

Night Visitors, Rayna Gillman, 18″ × 18″

Newspaper Strips

1. Tear newspaper into strips, and place them on stretched, pinned fabric. The grain of the newspaper and the direction in which you tear will determine the shape and size of the paper pieces. Sometimes you will get strips, other times, curves.

Curved newspaper strips

Fabric printed with curved newspaper strips

Straight newspaper strips

2. Lay the blank screen on top of the newspaper strips, and squeegee paint across the screen. The paint will cause the newspaper to stick to the screen so you can print again.

Results from first printing

3. Move the screen to a different part of the fabric, and repeat.

You can move the screen randomly, and print with as many colors as you like. With this method, there is no reason to worry about registration; you get what you get.

Print once, turn the screen the other way, and add another color.

Two-color printing with newspaper strips

As in the quilt below, placing newspaper strips on the fabric in a crosshatch pattern will give you squares or diamonds.

Solstice, Rayna Gillman, 13½″ × 21¼″

More with Strips

Okay, so you've printed several times with the newspaper strips. By now they are attached to the screen, but you're ready to move on and print something else. Before you do, be sure you get the most out of your newspaper and paint!

After you have finished printing, carefully lift the paper from the screen. The paint that remains on the paper will make another print if you lay the pieces on the fabric and roll a brayer over the strips.

Roll a brayer over the painted newspaper strips.

Peel the strips from the cloth, and voilà—a transparent effect!

It often pays to use the leftover strips; you don't waste the paint and can end up with some interesting, unplanned images.

In *Red Zone*, using up leftover newspaper strips helped turn a perfectly dreadful scrap of fabric into the cornerstone of a new piece.

Red Zone (detail), Rayna Gillman, (full quilt on page 21)

Newspaper Shapes

You can get more elaborate by cutting or tearing specific shapes out of paper and using the positive and/or negative spaces for a design.

For the piece below, I tore a paper doll out of newspaper and used the negative space as a stencil.

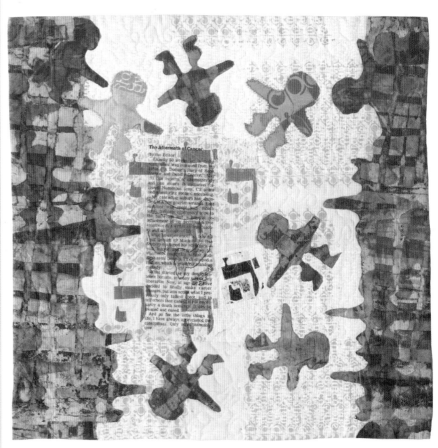

Semicolon, Rayna Gillman, 22½″ × 22½″

FREEZER-PAPER STENCILS

Freezer paper is more durable than newspaper. You can iron it to the screen or to the fabric and use it numerous times without having it fall apart.

Freezer Paper on Screens

Cut out random shapes from freezer paper, and iron them with the shiny side to the back (flat side) of the screen. This allows you to turn the design in various directions as you print.

Place the shiny side of the freezer paper against the screen when you iron.

Use the screen in any direction.

You can also cut freezer paper slightly larger than the screen mesh and cut shapes out of it before you iron it to the screen.

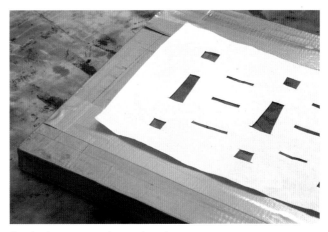

Cut the freezer paper larger than the screen.

When you've finished with the stencil, pull it off the screen, lay it face down on the fabric, and roll the brayer over it to get a negative print.

Positive print

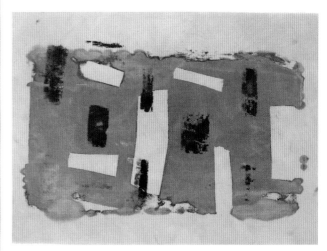

Negative print

Red Storm Rising, Pauline Salzman, 20½″ × 16½″

The black and white rectangles in the quilt above are positive and negative screenprints from a freezer-paper stencil.

Freezer Paper on Fabric

If you don't want a repeated image, ironing freezer paper to the fabric is the answer.

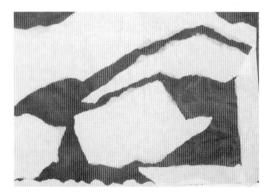

Iron freezer paper directly to the fabric.

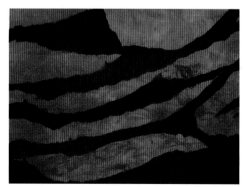

Use torn freezer paper for an organic look.

FOUND-OBJECT STENCILS

Items with spaces or holes in them work especially well when you are screenprinting. Any kind of grid can be effective; experiment to see what you prefer. If the item is completely flat, the screen will keep it in place while you work.

An easy way to start is to experiment with sequin waste and a screen. Sequin waste is metallic ribbon with holes punched in it, available in the florist supply or ribbon departments of some craft stores.

Sequin waste

Depending on your approach, it will yield varied results. If you put a piece of sequin waste between the fabric and the screen, and use it as a stencil, the paint will go through the holes and you'll get dots.

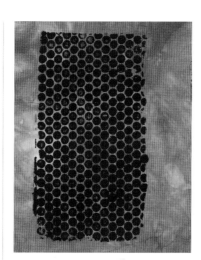

Use sequin waste as a stencil.

After you print, carefully remove the sequin waste and put it aside, paint side up. You will see an imprint remaining on the screen. Lay the screen down on the fabric, and squeegee over the remaining paint without adding anything; you'll get a different image.

Screen the resulting imprint.

Finally, put the sequin waste paint side down on the fabric, and roll a brayer over it, using it as a stamp. You'll get a negative print.

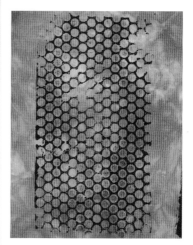

Use the sequin waste as a stamp to get a negative print.

The beauty of this process is that you can choose the effect you like best and do it again. Will it look exactly the same next time? No. But that's the point of printing spontaneously.

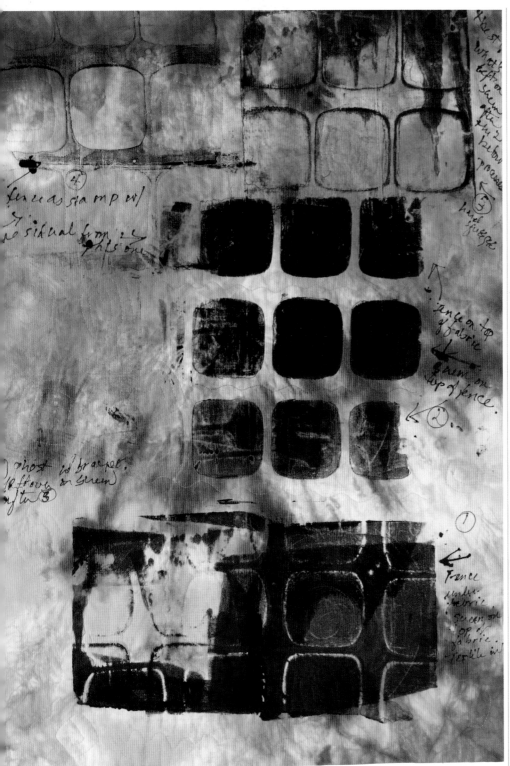

Artist's Proof, Rayna Gillman, 24˝ x 30˝

"WHAT IF?" VARIATIONS

Using a screen, a squeegee, and a brayer, you can get multiple images from the same item—all different, as you will see. It depends on how you use your tools.

In *Artist's Proof*, playing with construction fence and screens, I made a test piece to see what would happen if I put the fence under the screen on top of the cloth, under the cloth, printed with the residue in the screen, and finally used the fence as a stamp the way we did with the sequin waste. The handwriting was added with a syringe.

Here's an example of the process:

Put a piece of plastic fence under the screen, and use a squeegee to move the paint across the screen.

Put the resist (fence) under the screen.

But what if too much paint goes through and you have a lot of excess on the fabric?

Too much paint

It's a shame to waste that extra paint, so what if you were to lay a piece of cloth face down on top and run the brayer over it?

Ghost print from excess paint

What if you printed what was left in the screen? Then, what if you took the plastic fence from the screen, put it paint side down on the fabric, and used it as a stamp? And what if you left the piece of fence on the fabric and rolled over it with the paint-covered brayer? In the end it might look like the fabric at right.

Textured plates for rubbings can also give you beautiful results when you put them under the screen and squeegee over them.

Leaves, Denissa Schulman, 16½″ × 16″

GLUE RESISTS AS STENCILS

Yes, glue. Blue school glue gel is a great screen resist, and it washes out with soap and water. White school glue will also work if you don't have any blue glue gel on hand, but it is not as easy to get out of the screen.

Lay the screen on the table, flat side (back of screen) up. Apply the glue in any pattern you like, and let it dry for several hours or overnight.

Apply blue school glue.

You can speed up the drying process if you put the screen in the sun, or if you use a hair dryer. When the glue has dried, lay the screen on your stretched fabric, and print.

Your results can be varied and dramatic, depending on your design and how you apply the glue.

The glue is semipermanent, so it may begin to dissolve as you repeat the screening process. You will get slight variations in those areas. The rest should wash out with detergent, hot water, and a sponge. If some glue remains in the screen, take it in stride: it will become an accidental part of the next print!

tip *If you dedicate a screen to glue resist printing, you can leave the glue in the screen until you are ready to work.*

Remember not to let the paint dry in the screen or it will clog. Wash out the paint when you have finished printing with it. The glue will also wash out, so make sure you've pulled as many prints as you want with the same screen before you wash it.

SOY WAX RESISTS AS STENCILS

Chapter 7 is devoted to soy wax, and we will go into more detail there. Like glue, soy wax is semipermanent and will wash out with hot water and detergent, so you can also use it for screenprinting.

gelatin plate printing

Gelatin plate printing is a low-tech method that's not only fun and easy, it requires no special equipment beyond some unflavored gelatin from the supermarket and a foil pan. Artists love printing this way, and it is a wonderful activity to do with children of all ages.

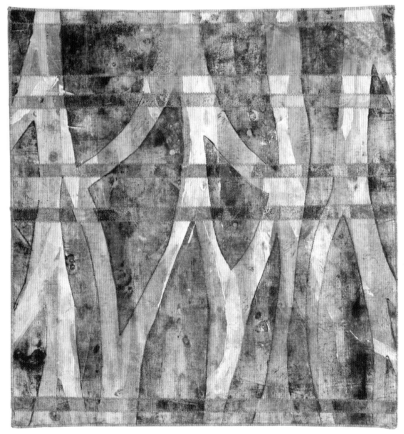

Forest Cathedral, Cornelia Jutta Forster, 13″ × 16″

why gelatin instead of an acrylic plate?

I've been asked this dozens of times and my answer is always the same: "You'll see." Some reasons to use a gelatin plate include the following:

- Gelatin is flexible and resilient in a way that other materials are not.
- Its rubbery texture picks up detail amazingly well.

- You can reuse it without cleaning it off.
- It becomes more interesting as it breaks down, adding texture to your work.
- You can cut it into pieces and rearrange it.
- You can stamp on it.
- It feels good under your hands.
- It's a great way to keep kids entertained.

supplies

- Unflavored gelatin
- Measuring cup
- Measuring spoons
- 1 plastic spoon
- Aluminum foil pans (8″ × 8″, 9″ round, or 9″ × 13″)
- Assorted found objects
- Freezer paper
- Foam plate or meat tray palette
- Assorted colors of textile paints
- Brayer
- Foam brush
- Notched spreader or faux painting comb

recipe:

making a gelatin plate

This recipe makes one 8″ × 8″ square plate. For a 9″ × 13″ plate, double the recipe.

- 4 envelopes or 4 tablespoons of unflavored gelatin
- 8″ × 8″ square foil cake pan
- 1 cup cool water
- 1 cup very hot or boiling water

directions

1. Put the gelatin into the foil pan.

2. Add the cool water all at once, and stir until the gelatin is dissolved. The mixture will be thick.

3. Add the hot or boiling water. Stir gently until the bubbles disappear from the surface. The mixture should be clear.

4. Put the foil pan into the refrigerator, and leave for about 30 minutes, or until firm.

 To avoid spills, use a cookie sheet to carry the foil pan and place it into the fridge.

When the gelatin is ready, run your finger or a knife around the edges of the pan, gently lift the gelatin out, and put it on a layer of plastic or freezer paper. It should come out easily. Don't worry if it is not perfect; it is not supposed to be perfect.

 Experiment with a round cake pan or pie tin for variety.

monoprinting
MONOPRINTING WITH FOUND OBJECTS

You can use anything flat with open areas. Plastic garden or construction fence works well, too.

The center of this piece was printed with a cardboard grid from one of my grandson's games, and a mesh onion bag.

1. Put about a teaspoon of paint onto the plate.

Put paint on the gelatin plate.

 It is better to start with less paint and add more if you need it. If the paint is too thick you will get globs on the fabric.

2. Roll out a thin coat of paint with a brayer. If it is too thick, remove some, and roll again.

Roll the paint onto the plate with a brayer.

3. Now you're ready to go.

After you have applied the paint, you can use ordinary tools to make extraordinary monoprints! Here are a few tools to try; you are bound to discover others as you explore the process.

I chose a piece of construction fencing to place on the painted gelatin. The grid acts as a resist so paint will not print in these areas.

1. Place the object on the gelatin plate.

 When you use a gelatin plate many times, it acquires cracks and scratches that give the prints added texture. This is a good thing!

2. Lay down the fabric, and press or smooth the fabric firmly against the plate using your hands or a brayer.

3. There is something delicious about the feel of the gelatin under your hands, although there are times you will want to use a brayer. Try using your hands first—it will bring out your inner kindergartener.

4. Now comes the fun part! Lifting the fabric is like opening a surprise package.

5. The first print, or positive, is from the gelatin plate with the grid still on it. Where the object has covered the paint, there are white lines.

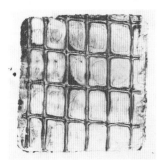

6. Carefully remove the object from the plate. The paint has remained where the grid was, and you can print at least once more.

7. Place another piece of fabric onto the plate, and press. The next print will be the second, or negative, print, which is even more interesting.

variations on a theme
MORE FOUND OBJECTS

Remember what we said in an earlier chapter about printing in layers? If you are not happy with what you print the first time around, just add more! This time, we're going to transform some muslin we had already printed with red, by laying the fabric on a blue gelatin plate and using a scrap of rubber with holes to block out some of the paint.

Place the rubber on a painted gelatin plate.

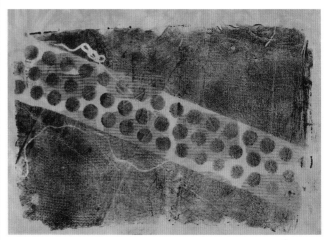

Variation 1: Print onto the already printed muslin. We've added transparency and texture—including a thread that got in the way and acted as an unintended resist. *Oops!* Does that bother us? Of course not! The more texture, the merrier.

Carefully lift the rubber from the plate, flip it over, and lay it across another area of the plate. There is still paint on both the gelatin and the flip side of the rubber, so we can print again with a different piece of cloth.

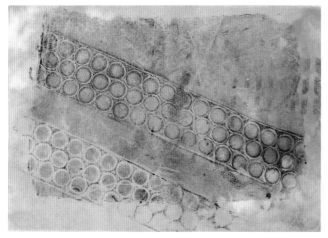

Variation 2: Here is the ghost, or second, monoprint made from the plate above.

The possibilities are limited only by your imagination!

LEAVES

Nature supplies us with some of the best found objects for printing. Leaves, twigs, and even flowers make good resists because gelatin picks up detail so well.

 Look for leaves with strong veins or other texture. When you use them for printing, place them face up on the gelatin plate because backs have more texture.

Ferns, Cornelia Jutta Forster, 8″ × 13½″

Here is what happens when we start to play with a delicate fern.

1. Apply paint to the gelatin plate with a brayer, and place the fern face up on the plate.

2. First print: a feathery silhouette, since the fern acted as a resist

5. A faint ghost remains on the gelatin. Print again and the cloth will pick it up. Because the print is faint, you can enhance it later by overprinting.

6. For the last print, take the fern, which still has paint on it, and place it paint side up on the gelatin. Print again and the paint will transfer.

3. Gently remove the fern from the gelatin, and put it aside, paint side up. The imprint of the back of the fern remains on the plate.

The possibilities are infinite. Experiment with leaves of all shapes, including plastic or skeleton leaves from the craft store. Use multiple leaves, multiple colors, and multiple items on one plate. In the fabric below, Patricia Smith used gelatin printing, rubbings (pages 80–84), and screenprinting (pages 21–32).

4. Second print: a beautifully detailed image. The second print is always my favorite, but each is wonderful in its own way and these make an interesting series.

Fabric by Patricia Smith

adding paint to the gelatin plate

There is no end to the ways you can use physical resists such as household items and natural objects, but there are still other ways to work with a gelatin plate.

ADDING PAINT WITH BRUSHES

If you paint, you can certainly use the gelatin plate as a canvas for monoprinting and do figurative sketching with a brush. This is not my strong suit, but if it is yours you might want to try it because the images pick up differently than they would on a rigid plate.

Print made from applying paint directly onto the gelatin plate

Fabric printed with a hand-carved circular stamp

ADDING PAINT WITH STAMPS

Far more interesting, I think, is the result you get when you add paint to the blank gelatin by stamping. Why stamp on the gelatin plate instead of directly onto fabric?

- You can ink once, then stamp numerous times. Paint remains on the stamp because gelatin is not absorbent.

- You can get at least two prints from one stamped plate.

- The fabric will pick up not only the stamp pattern, but texture from the plate. If the gelatin is starting to crack, so much the better!

1. Spread paint on a stamp, and stamp onto the gelatin.

2. Here is the first print.

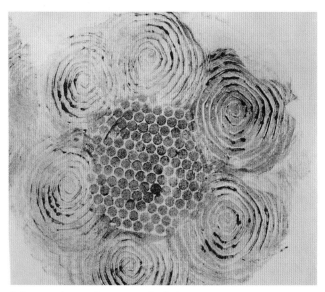

3. For the second print, add a circle of sequin waste to the plate, and dab some paint into the center.

4. Remove the sequin waste and print!

removing paint from the gelatin plate

REMOVING PAINT USING STAMPS

The results are striking when you roll paint onto the plate and then stamp into it, removing some of the pigment and making a negative imprint. You can use almost anything as a stamp: found objects as well as commercial or hand-carved stamps.

Use a potato masher as a stamp.

When you print, the overlapped circles seem almost three-dimensional and have detail you can't get with any other method.

REMOVING PAINT USING OTHER METHODS

If you prefer, you can simply roll paint onto the plate, and remove some to create abstract designs, stripes, or wavy lines.

Use a notched spreader or faux painting tool, and pull it across the gelatin plate.

First print and second (or ghost) print

Before you print again, lay an item on the plate. Your next print will be more complex, and you will have begun to create transparency and layers.

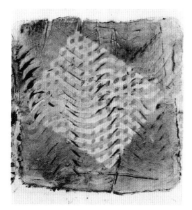

Plastic grid used as resist

paper resists

Experiment with paper towels, waxed paper, or freezer paper on a gelatin plate. One day, feeling especially playful, I cut some freezer-paper stencils and laid them on a gelatin plate. While these results were just plain fun, you can create some interesting abstractions if you experiment by moving the stencils around and overprinting.

Experimental freezer-paper stencils

deconstructing the gelatin plate

Gelatin plates fall apart sooner or later depending on a variety of factors: the thickness of the gelatin plate, the quality of the gelatin, and how much or how hard you have used the plate. Working organically and letting the plate take the lead, so to speak, can lead you in new directions.

Broken gelatin plate

If you print two pieces of cloth with the same broken pieces, using two different paint colors, the results will be similar in texture. However, they can be entirely different in feeling.

This one, printed in browns, reminded me of an old wall, and I followed that lead when I added another layer.

First layer

With the addition of some hieroglyphic text, the print became ancient parchment. I used a Thermofax screen (more about these on page 89), but I could easily have used a commercial rubber stamp with text on it.

Second layer

The same broken pieces painted in an icy blue said "winter" and became a backdrop for the overprinted trees.

oops!

Serendipity raises its head occasionally and gifts us with unintended design opportunities. Most of what we create here is accidental, and it is very freeing not to worry about making it perfect.

I call this "I couldn't have done it if I had tried." Come along with me while I take advantage of some gelatin blobs.

I had put a pie plate into the fridge to gel, and when I retrieved it I found that the liquid gelatin had leaked onto the shelf and had hardened into the shapes of the spill. I peeled the shapes from the refrigerator shelf, painted them, added a couple of stamped flourishes, and printed.

Organic gelatin print

Over-dyed, and with some added circles, this is how the piece looked later.

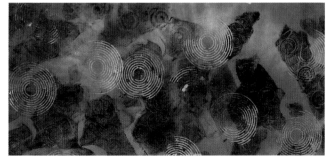

Circles stamped and screened on fabric

One of my early gelatin print experiments was rather murky. It brightened considerably when I screened with gold paint.

Murky fabric brightened with gold paint

As broken pieces or a whole plate, gelatin makes a versatile background for additional texture, color, text, and images.

Linda Witte Henke used a pencil eraser and mesh to stamp and embellish her gelatin-printed piece.

Bar None, Linda Witte Henke, 13″ × 16½″

Cornelia Jutta Forster takes a different approach by cutting her gelatin-printed cloth into pieces and reassembling them into beautiful fiber collages.

All of the fabric in the quilt below was monoprinted on a gelatin plate using acrylic paint, except for one piece of fabric hand dyed by Helene Davis.

Illumination, Cornelia Jutta Forster, 11˝ × 18˝

River Rocks, Laura Cater Woods, 15˝ × 23½˝

screenprinting with thickened dyes

This is not a book about dyeing fabric; you can find any number of excellent books on that subject. But you don't need to know how to dye fabric to screen, stamp, paint, or draw with thickened dyes. This is a foolproof, forgiving way to use dyes.

supplies

See Supplies and Sources on page 94 for sources of supplies.

- Procion MX dyes
- Pro Dye Activator or soda ash
- Water
- Pro Thick SH or sodium alginate
- Silkscreen
- Squeegees
- Plastic measuring spoons
- Dust mask or respirator
- Rubber gloves
- Plastic or glass measuring cups
- Newspaper
- Urea

Optional but good to have:

- Reduran (to remove dye from your hands)
- Hair dryer (for drying screens quickly)
- Painting tools such as brushes and syringe
- Stockpot for steaming fabric to set the dye

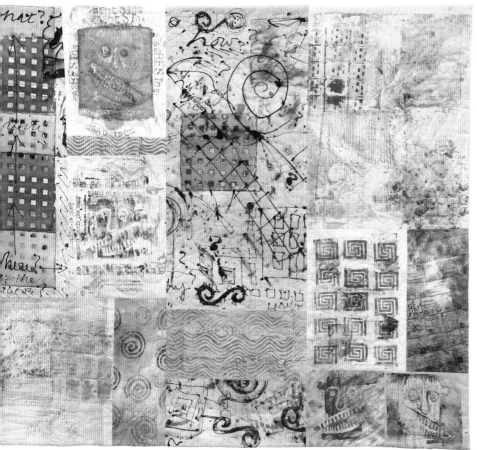

Urban Landscape, Rayna Gillman, 40″ × 34″

why thickened dyes?

The beauty of thickened dyes is their versatility. Unlike paint, dye penetrates the fabric without changing the hand, and can be over-dyed or discharged to modify or remove (discharge) color. Thickened dyes won't clog the screen, and you can use them on silk, which gives you a flexibility you don't have with paint.

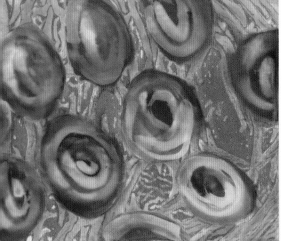

**Deconstructed printing on silk fabric
by Kerr Grabowski**

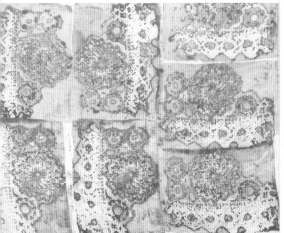

**Deconstructed printing on silk fabric
by Diane Savona**

print now or later

We will look at two ways to print with these dyes. Depending on your mood, you can print immediately or let the dye dry in the screen, and print the next day or even a few weeks later. Each has its merits and each will give you totally different results.

Following are the recipes you will need to print with thickened dyes. Once you mix them, they will last for several weeks as long as you do not add soda ash or dye activator. Some people find that the dyes last longer when they are refrigerated, so it can't hurt. However, I have kept the thickened dyes at room temperature for a few weeks without problem.

Soda ash or Dye Activator is used to set the dyes. You can soak fabric in soda ash, you can add soda ash to the thickened dyes, or you can make your prints with soda ash paste (page 47).

safety guidelines

Use common sense when working with dyes and chemicals: wear rubber gloves, old clothes, and a disposable dust mask while you work with dye powder. Here are some basics:

- Cover your work area with newspaper, and spray to dampen it while you are mixing dyes.
- Use glass or plastic measuring cups and plastic spoons to measure and stir.
- Wipe up spills before they dry to a powder.
- Clearly label all dyes and other solutions.

 ProChem has excellent safety and disposal guidelines on its website (www.prochemical.com).

print paste recipes

Clear print paste is used to make thickened dyes. Soda ash paste is used to release colored dye paste from the screen. I recommend making a quart at a time of print paste and dividing it in half, filling two pint-size plastic containers.

clear print paste

1. Measure 1 quart of hot (110°) water into a plastic container. Add 9 tablespoons of urea and dissolve.

2. Sprinkle 2–4 rounded tablespoons of sodium alginate into the water while stirring rapidly. (A small whisk is good for this.)

3. Continue stirring until the paste is smooth. It will become smoother if you let it stand 1 hour or overnight.

4. Divide the clear print paste into 2 pint containers. Label 1 container CLEAR PRINT PASTE. This is the base to which you will add dye powder.

You can store print paste in a closed container for up to 6 months.

 Print paste will be very thick. It should be about the consistency of yogurt, so add water a little at a time to thin it if you wish.

recipe: soda ash paste

1. To the other pint container of print paste, add 1 tablespoon of soda ash or Pro Dye Activator dissolved in a little bit of warm water.

2. Label it clearly SODA ASH PASTE.

When you are screenprinting with dye paste that has dried on the screen, you will use this to release the colored dye paste from the screen.

While you are wearing your mask, mix several colors at one time. Once the powder has dissolved completely, you can remove your mask. Keep the gloves on while you work.

recipe: soda ash soak

1. Mix 9 tablespoons of soda ash in 1 gallon of hot water until dissolved. This will keep in a closed container.

2. Soak fabric in it for 5–20 minutes, and hang to dry. Do not put soda-ash-soaked fabric in the dryer.

recipe: thickened dyes

1. Put on your dust mask and gloves. Measure dye powder into a container, and add a small amount of warm water to dissolve the dye into a thin paste.

2. Add thickened clear print paste (page 46), and stir until the dye is dissolved.

Use:
- 2 teaspoons dye powder for $^1/_4$ cup print paste
- 4 teaspoons dye powder for $^1/_2$ cup print paste
- 6 teaspoons dye powder for $^3/_4$ cup print paste
- 8 teaspoons dye powder for 1 cup print paste

The first time around, I recommend starting with the smallest quantity of dye powder and print paste. The recipe makes a dark, concentrated color, and you can easily lighten the color or extend the amount by adding clear print paste.

If you want to make your dye paste thinner, add water a little bit at a time, and stir until it is the consistency you are looking for. Thickened dye lasts for a long time, as long as you don't add soda ash to the mix.

This highly concentrated color should be diluted a bit with clear paste if you are doing immediate screenprinting. For deconstructed sceenprinting, use concentrated dye paste color as is.

immediate screenprinting

Once you've mixed the dye paste, you can print immediately. If your fabric has already been soaked in soda ash, you need only pull the thickened dye across the screen, just as you would with paint (pages 22–23). Once it has dried, you can print another layer of dye. Unlike paint, it will penetrate the cloth and create transparent layers. Immediate screenprinting is especially good with glue (page 32) and wax resists (pages 78–79).

Judy Langille printed several layers of dye on the fabric in this piece.

Torn Forms Blue, Judy Langille, 18″ × 24″

If the fabric has not been soaked in the soda ash solution, dissolve ½ teaspoon of soda ash in a bit of hot water, and add it to ½ cup of dye paste immediately before printing. Just be sure you use up all the dye paste containing soda ash within four hours, before it loses its potency.

 If you are adding soda ash, make ½ cup of dye paste at a time so you can use it all in one printing session.

deconstructed screenprinting

Admittedly, screening with thickened dye is immediate and yields beautiful results. But when you let the dye dry in the screen and print the next day, or even a week later, the results are entirely different; they are less pre- dictable and much more exciting. Textile artist and teacher Kerr Grabowski, who introduced me to the process, calls it deconstructed screenprinting because each time you print, more of the dye dissolves in the screen and moves onto the fabric. With a nod to Kerr, I call it deconstructed, but you could call it next-day dye printing because once you have let the thickened dyes dry in the screen, you can print with it the next day, or even the next week.

GETTING STARTED

One way to make a screen for deconstructed screen-printing is with a physical resist. Anything with holes or bumps will do: textured plastic plates from the art store, a sink mat, bubble wrap, doilies—whatever is within reach. Each will give you a different result.

PREPARING THE SCREEN

If you have textured plastic plates that art stores sell for doing rubbings, you might want to use one for your first deconstructed screen. They come in a variety of patterns.

Textured plastic plates are easy to start with.

1. Put down a layer of newspaper. Place the resist between the newspaper and the screen. Here, I am using a rubbing plate. Don't forget the gloves.

2. Use colored dye paste *without soda ash,* and squeegee paste across until the screen is covered.

The dye adheres to the screen where the plastic touches it.

3. Put the screen aside, flat side up, and let it dry completely. You can leave it in the sun or indoors for several hours, days, or weeks.

If you want instant gratification, you can dry the screen with a hair dryer.

Depending on the thickness of your dye and the kind of resist you are using, dried screens will look different from one another and will print differently.

Because the dye paste on the screen on the right is thicker and darker, you will get many more prints from this screen than from the one on the left.

MAKING THE PRINT

Stretch and pin your fabric tightly so it does not move when you lift the screen.

Once the screen is completely dry, place it flat side down on the pinned fabric.

Spoon the soda ash paste onto the edge of the screen.

Squeegee the paste across the screen.

It may take a minute or two and a few vigorous passes of the gel until the dried dye loosens up and goes through to the fabric. The longer the dye has been in the screen, the longer it will take for the dye to loosen and print with the first pass. If you have left it for weeks, you will need to let the print paste sit for a while on the screen to dissolve some of the dry dye.

Peek to see what has printed.

After the first pass, pick up the end of the screen, and peek at the fabric to see what has printed. If you see that some dye is coming through, but not enough, replace the screen, and keep printing. Move the screen, and print again.

The dye will come out through the blank areas on the screen, giving you a negative print. You will notice that the once-clear gel picks up the color from the screen as it deposits the dye onto the fabric.

The first print may not be this distinct.

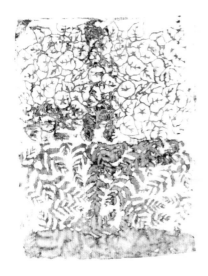

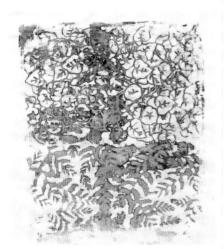

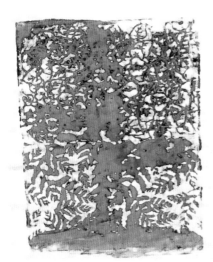

As the print paste releases the dye from the screen, it gets more complex.

Move the screen, and repeat the screenprinting process. By the time you have made four to six prints, most of the pattern may have disappeared from the screen. Continue until there is almost no dye left on the screen.

By the end, there will be little dye left on the screen.

 This is a messy process: wear gloves, add more clear soda ash paste as you need it, and squeegee in all directions.

 Excess soda ash paste from the screen can go into a separate plastic container to be reused. However, because it now contains dye it will give you a different result from clear soda ash paste, adding to the variety of your prints.

When you use more than one resist on a screen, you will get a more complex print.

For the red and white fabric in the piece below, I used several resists at once to make the screen.

You can use almost anything with texture to make a deconstructed screen. Leaves were the resist that made this feathery print.

Portrait, Rayna Gillman, 12¼˝ × 13¼˝

Greetings From Augusta, Judy Carpenter, 15˝ × 22˝

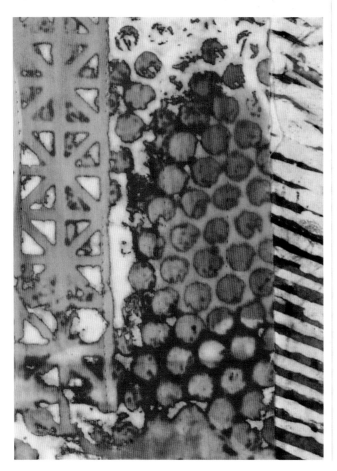

Here are four strike-offs from the same screen. Notice how the print changes as more dye is released. Each is unique, yet they are all related. Notice that by the last print, the screen is almost completely empty of dye. This is as it should be when you are finished.

Print 1

Print 2

Print 3

Print 4

Early Frost, Rayna Gillman, 35″ × 32″

Several pieces of deconstructed fabric are used in this quilt.

making your mark on the screen

A wonderful, freeing way to print is to write, scribble, doodle, or draw on the screen with thickened dyes using brushes, a syringe, or anything else you choose. Draw pictures, make circles, doodle, or write. This is *really* fun, and your print will be as individual as your handwriting because this is the work of your hand.

Kerr created her scarf by drawing and doodling on the screen, then printing.

*Scarf #507,
Kerr Grabowski,
15" × 72"*

Below is fabric that has been printed with a doodled-on screen. Along the way, I added a drop of yellow print paste to the clear paste, just to see what would happen. Have fun, and experiment with this process.

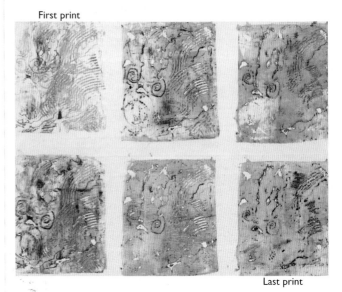

First print

Last print

cleaning the screen

Dye is easier to remove from screens than paint because it doesn't clog the pores. Wash dyes out of screens with soap, warm water, and a sponge. Some colors may stain the screen, but that doesn't interfere with the printing.

setting the dye

BATCHING VS. STEAMING

Batching and steaming are two different methods for setting the dyes; each has its advocates. Most people who work with dyes use the batching method; I prefer to steam. Either way will give you good results.

Batching

To batch your dyed fabric, cover the printed fabric with plastic, and let it sit overnight. Then soak the fabric in a bucket of cold water, changing the water several times. This will prevent excessive washout of the dye. Then machine wash the fabric in hot water and Synthrapol.

Steaming

You don't really need to steam MX dyes, but I steam my deconstructed fabrics because I believe there is less washout and that colors are more vivid when I steam, especially on silk. I either hang my fabric to dry or, if I am in a big hurry, use a hair dryer. Since steaming is neither difficult nor expensive, I will share my method with you.

Note: The fabric must be dry before you steam it.

1. Buy an inexpensive spaghetti, or stockpot—20 quarts is a good size. If you have a colander that will fit inside the pot, turn it upside down and put it on the bottom. Or, use an aluminum foil angel food cake pan turned upside down with holes punched in the bottom. The foil pan will last through many, many steamings. Add 1″–2″ of water to the pot.

Prepare the stockpot for steaming.

2. Cut a dozen or more 9″–10″ circles from newspaper. Lay 6 to 8 of them on the upside-down colander or cake pan.

3. Cover the table with newspaper, and place your fabric on top. Make sure the layers of newspaper are larger than your fabric.

Place the fabric on top of newspaper.

4. Fold the edge of the newspaper over the fabric, and keep folding until the fabric is wrapped and looks like a long tube. You may want to secure the long edge of the newspaper with tape.

Fold the newspaper over the fabric.

5. Fold one end of the tube over twice.

Fold the end of the tube.

6. You can accordion-fold it and use rubber bands to keep it together—my preferred method.

Fold in the ends of the newspaper.

Accordion-folded newspaper

As you finish, fold the last end inside the package. If you have more than one package, you can stack them.

Or you can roll it until it is coiled and then tape the end with masking tape.

Coil the folded newspaper.

7. Place the folded or rolled package in the pot.

Place the package on the newspaper circles in the pot.

8. Then put the other 6 newspaper circles on top of the packages, put the lid on the pot, and steam for 20 minutes.

9. Lift the packages out with tongs, unwrap, and rinse in cold water; then wash in hot water and Synthrapol.

tip *Do not let the newspaper circles or the fabric packages touch the edges of the pot.*

working in layers

Deconstructed screenprinting lends itself to working in layers because, by its very nature, it involves peeling away layers of dye as you work. It is easy to use several screens in succession without obliterating the previous strata. This gives your cloth complexity, even though the process itself is simple.

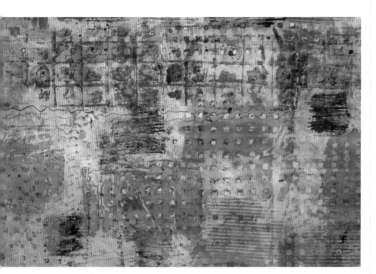

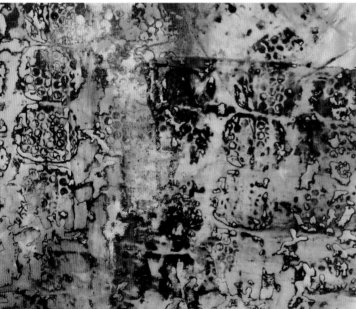

The above examples show how you can build complexity by printing with several screens in succession.

Of course, if you want to change the cloth further, you can use discharge paste or bleach gels in your screen to remove some of the color. Chapter 6 (starting on page 58) looks at the discharge process in more detail, but in the meantime, here is an example that was deconstructed with discharge paste instead of clear print paste.

Deconstructed with discharge paste

With deconstructed screenprinting, like everything else we are working with, the possibilities are limited only by your imagination. Keep asking "what if?" and let your imagination guide you as you work.

discharge printing

Removing color from fabric (better known as discharging) is a combination of art, serendipity, and chemistry that is sometimes frustrating. But don't let that stop you from trying it, because you can create beautiful fabric with discharge.

supplies

- Discharge paste or Thiox
- Products containing chlorine bleach in gel form, such as dishwashing or cleaning gels
- Anti-Chlor (sodium bisulfite)
- Foam brushes
- Respirator made for filtering gas fumes
- Gloves

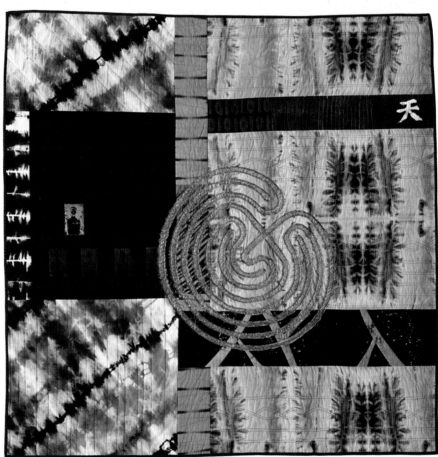

The Caldron, Linda Colsh, 51″ × 51″

While discharging can give you exciting results, it is probably the quirkiest, least predictable method for changing the surface of fabric. The variables are almost infinite. The examples on the next page are commercial black fabrics discharged with a variety of agents. What a difference!

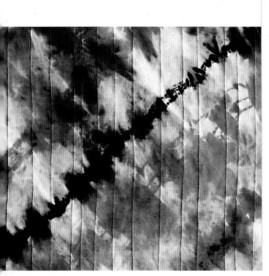

Discharge paste on fabric from two different manufacturers

Thiox on fabric from two different bolts from the same manufacturer

Chlorine bleach on fabric from two different manufacturers

types of discharge agents

Several types of chemicals remove color from fabric. Chlorine bleach is the one you will probably think of first. It is most readily available and works quickly, but it is hardest on fabric and cannot be used on silk.

Discharge paste and Thiox (thiourea dioxide, available from ProChem and other sources) are activated by steam and will not destroy fabric. Both are safe to use on silk. We will go into more detail on all of these discharge agents, starting on page 61.

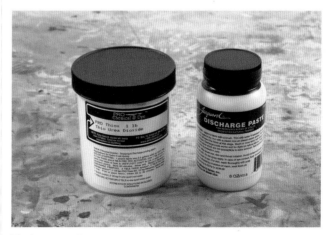

Discharge products

safety guidelines

Before you begin, know that you will need to pay special attention to safety guidelines when you discharge, *no matter which type of discharge agent you use.*

- Work outside or in a well-ventilated area.
- Wear a respirator made for filtering gas fumes.
- Wear gloves and old clothes.
- Always neutralize bleached fabric.

expect the unexpected

Depending on the fabric, the discharge agent, the method, the temperature, the humidity, the timing, and possibly the phases of the moon, you can get entirely different results, or no results.

No results? Discharging can usually remove color from dyed fabric, but not always. Some dyes are so colorfast that they will not discharge; certain commercially dyed fabrics will react with bleach but not with discharge paste, or vice versa. Three different chlorine bleach household products were used below.

Left to right: results from dishwasher gel, bleach pen, Soft Scrub

Chlorine products used to discharge fabric

After being rinsed, neutralized, and washed, the blue color (center) disappeared completely, and the cloth returned to almost black, barely discharged.

If you are discharging black fabric, you never know what you will get. Black differs by brand and even by bolt because manufacturers often over-dye other colors to get black. As a result, you will often see the original color of the fabric, depending on your choice of discharge method.

Thiox revealed a gray-green under the black.

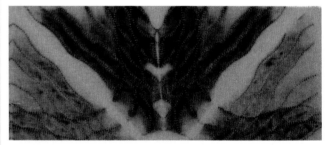

This black linen became tan.

chlorine bleach products

You may not think twice about the safety of chlorine bleach because you probably have it in your home. Keep in mind that when you use it in your laundry, you are adding only a small amount to a full washing machine, so it is extremely diluted. However, bleach is a dangerous substance with toxic fumes. For this reason, I do not recommend using *liquid* bleach. If you insist on removing color with bleach, be sure you dilute it at least to 1 part bleach to 4–8 parts water, and observe the safety guidelines noted above: gloves, respirator, good ventilation (it is best to work outdoors), and neutralizing the fabric afterward to stop the bleaching action (see below).

 Never use chlorine bleach on silk; it will destroy the fabric. Use it only on cotton or rayon.

BLEACH GELS

Dishwasher gels, bleach pens, and blue cleanup gel cleaners have less potent fumes and a smaller risk of spills because the chlorine has been thickened and diluted with other ingredients. If you are careful, these are easy, inexpensive, accessible products for removing color. Nevertheless, you must still neutralize the fabric.

Discharged fabrics and commercial fabrics are artfully combined in Linda Colsh's quilt *Rage and Outrage I.*

Rage and Outrage I, Linda Colsh, 48″ × 45″

NEUTRALIZING BLEACHED FABRIC

If you have ever used chlorine bleach on a piece of clothing to get the stains out, you know that eventually you may see small holes develop in the fabric. You do not want this to happen to your art! Bleach keeps working, even after you have washed it, unless you stop the action. Anti-Chlor (sodium bisulfite) is the only substance that stops chlorine bleach from destroying fabric.

Neither hydrogen peroxide nor vinegar (two old wives' tales) will do the job. Anti-Chlor is available from ProChem, and a similar product is available from other dye houses. It is inexpensive, and since you need only 1 teaspoon per 2½ gallons of water, one jar can last for years.

Step One: Rinse

After your fabric has reached the color you want, rinse or soak it thoroughly in cold water for at least 5 minutes. This will not stop the bleaching action, but it will remove enough bleach to prepare the fabric for soaking in neutralizer.

Step Two: Soak in Anti-Chlor

Thoroughly dissolve 1 teaspoon of Anti-Chlor in 1¼ gallons of hot water. Soak the discharged fabric for 5 minutes, stirring occasionally. That's all it takes.

Miriam Otte used a bleach pen to discharge the black fabric in this piece.

Missing Her, Miriam Otte, 28″ × 30″

VARIABLES

There are numerous variables that determine your results. The fabric below was screened with dishwasher gel. The variable was the length of time the gel sat on the fabric before it was rinsed, neutralized, and washed.

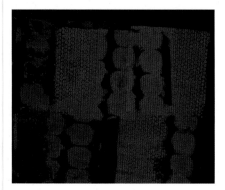

Dishwasher gel after 5 minutes

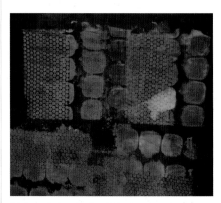

Dishwasher gel after 30 minutes

The variable in the next fabric was the discharge substance.

The circles are blue cleanup gel cleaner overlaid with lines of dishwasher gel.

In most cases, bleach products will give you various shades of orange to beige. Discharge paste and Thiox will give you more control and more variety, although the results are equally unpredictable.

discharge paste

In the end, this is a matter of personal choice, but many artists prefer discharge paste or Thiox over bleach products.

WHY USE DISCHARGE PASTE?

- It is safe to use on all fabrics, including silk. Because discharge paste does not weaken fibers, as chlorine bleach does, you do not need to neutralize. However, you do need to wear a respirator and take the same safety precautions as you would with bleach.

- You have more control over the results. Unlike bleach, which starts working as soon as you apply it, discharge paste needs heat and moisture to activate it. A steam iron is the most common method. Because *you* hold the iron, *you* control how much heat and moisture hit the fabric, and for how long. By experimenting, you can discharge some areas of the fabric more than others, if you wish, varying the results.

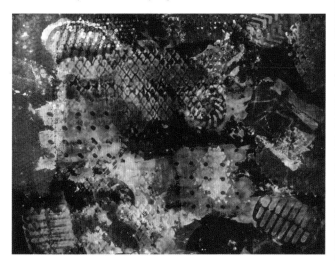

Discharge paste on black fabric

- There is a greater variety of discharged color. Rarely will you get orange when you use discharge paste, but you will see everything from pink to blue to turquoise to green to beige to pure white. It depends on the bolt, the manufacturer, and the color of the base fabric.

The center panel of the black fabric in *Blueprint* discharged to a remarkable turquoise with discharge paste. Rachel B. Cochran has never been able to duplicate this color, even with more fabric from the same manufacturer.

Blueprint, Rachel B. Cochran, 24½″ × 30½″

HOW TO USE DISCHARGE PASTE

While the manufacturer's instructions tell you to let the fabric dry and then steam iron it, I find it works better if you steam the fabric while the paste is still damp. Some other things I advise include the following:

- Wear a respirator, and/or do this outside. I cannot repeat this enough.

- Use an old iron that is dedicated to discharge.

- To avoid smearing if the paste is still damp, do not iron directly on the fabric. Hold the iron slightly above the fabric, and steam.

- If you let the discharge paste dry, put a layer of newspaper on top, spray it with water to saturate it, and iron. Keep spraying and steam ironing. Lift the paper frequently to check what is happening to the fabric's color so you can decide when to stop. When you use discharge paste, you can over-dye and discharge multiple times without weakening the fiber.

IT'S NOT JUST FOR BLACK

While black will give you the most dramatic results, discharge paste also works on hand-dyed and many (not all) colored commercial fabrics such as the red in this piece.

Tenement, Rayna Gillman, 17½˝ × 17½˝

A screen made with thickened dye was deconstructed onto this hand-dyed blue using discharge paste instead of soda ash paste (page 50). The discharge paste deposited the color on the screen at the same time it removed the color from the fabric.

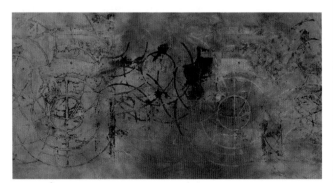

This hand-dyed fabric was deconstructed with discharge paste.

Discharge paste was put through a screen with a blue glue resist (page 32). Notice how many colors come through in this hand-dyed fabric by Helene Davis.

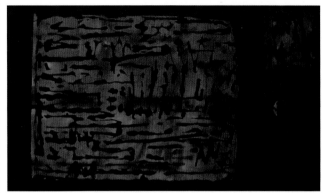

Fabric by Helene Davis

The hand-dyed brown fabric for *Echoes* discharged to yellow; dye was painted back into the fabric in places.

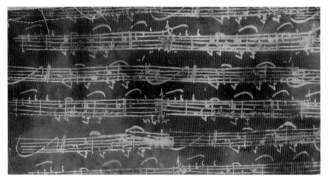

Echoes, Rayna Gillman, 36¾˝ × 37˝

Judy Langille painted her quilt with thickened dyes, over-dyed, and discharged multiple times to achieve a specific effect.

Diane Savona left the iron in place to make a discharged impression that is a focal point for this piece.

Torn Forms I, Judy Langille, 32″ × 40″

Treasure Hunt, Diane Savona, 19″ × 28¹/₂″

You can also discharge cloth that has been painted, but because the paint is a resist, only the unpainted areas will discharge. This process is a good remedy for a too-dark piece of fabric.

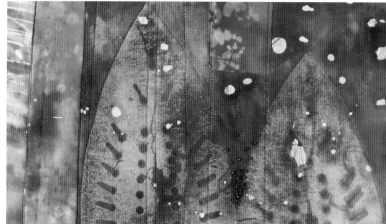

thiox

Thiox comes in powder form and gives similar results to discharge paste when mixed into a paste following the recipe on the jar. Thiox, available from dye suppliers, can be mixed and used like discharge paste, or you can follow the instructions on the jar to make a bath for discharging large pieces of fabric by boiling them. As with all discharge agents, Thiox should be used outside or in a well-ventilated area while you wear a respirator.

The top and bottom fabrics in the piece below were discharged in a Thiox bath.

This shirt was just another faded, stained black shirt until I threw it into a pot of Thiox and let it cook for a few minutes. Now it's a conversation piece.

Lost, Rayna Gillman, 17˝ × 23˝

the bottom line on discharge

I've mentioned that this is sometimes a frustrating process. But warned in advance, you can adjust your expectations.

- **Some colors will not discharge.** If you are using hand-dyed fabrics, keep in mind that turquoise, golden yellow, and fuchsia may get lighter, but they will not go away entirely. Turquoise may not change at all.

- **Some fabrics will not discharge.** No matter what you use, the color will not change. Or, if the fabric is not black, the color may actually darken when you bleach it. There is no sane explanation for this.

- **Some fabrics will discharge with bleach but not with discharge paste.** Or vice versa.

- **You may not like the color you get on a particular fabric.** You can over-dye or paint it.

- **You may get a color you love and never get it again.** This is par for the course. Two bolts from the same manufacturer may have different base colors.

So, the bottom line is this: go with the process and enjoy the accidental results. This can open a whole new avenue for you.

soy wax batik

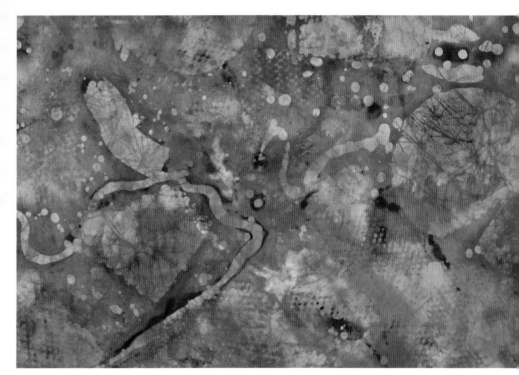

Whether you're new to batik or have used traditional wax and want to switch to nontoxic soy wax, you'll love this twenty-first-century approach to an ancient art. Soy wax, pigments, brushes, and household items are all you need to get started creating gorgeous fabrics.

a brief introduction to batik

Artists have used a mixture of paraffin and beeswax for centuries, with spectacular results. All over the world, batik fabrics are printed using traditional copper or wood stamps, traditional batik wax, and fiber-reactive dyes. Commercial batik fabrics are boiled in huge vats to remove the wax.

If you've ever spilled candle wax on a tablecloth, you know you can remove it by dry cleaning. Or you can boil the tablecloth till the wax comes out. Neither is a happy prospect. Many fiber artists who work in smaller quantities send their fabrics to the dry cleaner. However, the older dry-cleaning chemicals that remove wax are being replaced by newer, less toxic chemicals that don't do the same job. And many artists don't want the dry-cleaning expense or exposure to chemicals if they can find an alternative. Enter soy wax as a substitute.

soy wax

Developed originally to create candles that are environmentally better than petrochemical wax candles, soy wax is readily available in bulk via the Internet from a growing number of candle suppliers. Depending on the source, you will see soy wax labeled as "pure soy wax," "container wax," "pillar wax," or "pillar/votive wax." You want the pillar or pillar/votive wax because it is harder than the container or pure soy wax. You can purchase it without guesswork from ProChem (see Supplies and Sources on page 94), which carries the exact mixture you will need for surface design.

safety guidelines

While soy wax is nontoxic and does not emit fumes you need to worry about, you still need to be careful about how you handle it. It melts at a lower temperature than traditional batik wax, so you need to keep your frying pan temperature at about 200°–225°. Some electric frying pans heat more quickly than others, so you need to get used to your own pan, and you may need to toggle it between 200° and a smidge higher.

Wax flakes beginning to melt. Wait for the wax to be completely clear to begin work.

Use salad tongs to lift flat objects from the hot wax.

Don't worry if the wax turns color after you have dipped in rusty or metal objects; this does not harm the wax and will not affect your results. But *do not let the wax smoke*, and do not leave the pan unattended. When you are finished, don't just turn off the temperature dial; unplug it from the pan, because it is too easy to turn the dial in the wrong direction when you mean to turn it to "off."

supplies

You don't need elaborate or expensive equipment to print with. Almost any metal, resin, or wood implement will work if it has a flat surface and will not melt in hot wax.

- Electric frying pan
- 1 pound or more of soy pillar wax
- Several inexpensive natural-bristle brushes of different sizes
- Foam brushes
- Metal salad tongs
- Spray bottle with water
- Metal, wood, or resin household objects such as a potato masher, a metal grid, children's wood blocks, etc.
- Textile paints
- MX dyes, soda ash, and sodium alginate
- Discharge paste (optional)
- Small electric wax pot (optional)
- Tjantings (optional)
- Wood stamps, copper tjaps (optional)
- Iron

Batik supplies

NONTRADITIONAL TOOLS

Many household tools will work well with wax, as long as they are made of materials that don't melt. Children's wood blocks, old metal linotype letters, potato mashers, and spatulas are all possibilities. Metal implements or items made of resin (a plastic-like material that doesn't melt) are all fine. Rubber stamps are not a good idea since the heat can melt the adhesive.

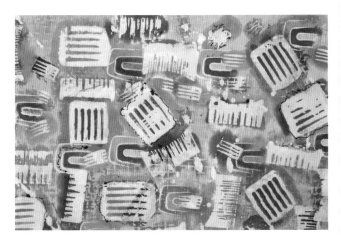

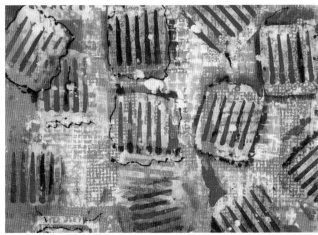

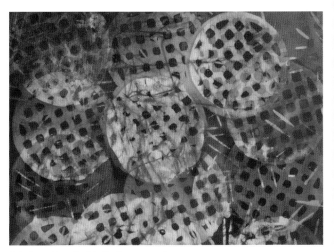

Fabrics printed with kitchen utensils

The centerpiece of this art quilt was printed with kitchen objects and rusty metal from a scrap heap.

Empowered, Marlene Cohen, 26½″ × 48″

Diane Savona's work incorporates fabric printed with soy wax resist, wire grids, and kitchen utensils.

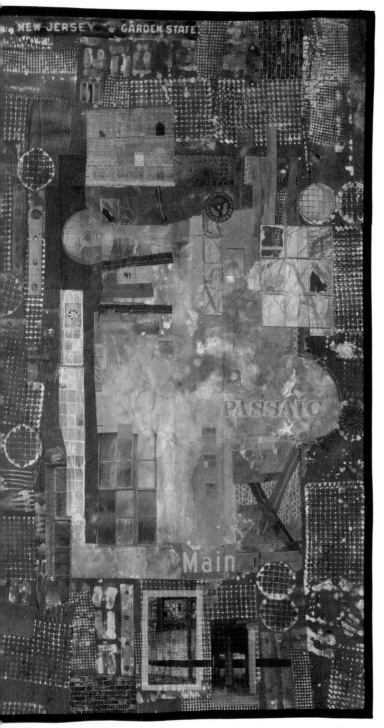

Road Cloth: Factory Windows, Diane Savona, 35″ × 62″

TRADITIONAL COPPER STAMPS (TJAPS)

Copper heats more quickly and holds heat longer than any other material. As with any stamp you are using with wax, let the excess wax drip back into the pot before you use the stamp. This will ensure a clearer impression on the fabric. The heavier the stamp and the more complex the design, the more wax it will hold and the more impressions you can make before it runs out of wax. Don't worry if your first few stampings with a heavy, complex tjap are indistinct because there is so much wax. These will enable you to make a wonderful crackle pattern; just scrunch the fabric before you add paint or dye.

Copper tjap and printed batik cloth

TRADITIONAL WOOD STAMPS

Wood stamps are widely available and are less expensive than copper. The designs range from simple to elaborate. The wood stamps that you find may have been used for printing fabric with dyes in India or Afghanistan.

Afghan wood stamp

While wood stamps can be used with wax, wood does not heat as quickly as metal or retain heat, so you will probably get only one strong impression before you need to put it back into the wax.

BRUSHES AND TJANTINGS

Inexpensive, natural-bristle paintbrushes of different sizes make wonderful tools that let you make your own marks on the fabric with wax. Don't use brushes with synthetic bristles because they will melt.

1. Let your brush sit in the hot wax for a minute or two.

2. Remove the brush, and let the wax drip back into the pan. Make random marks on the fabric. Check to see that the wax has penetrated the fabric. If not, put the brush back, and repeat.

Tjantings are used by traditional batik artists for drawing, and enable you to make more delicate marks or write with wax. Copper tjantings keep the wax hot longer than other metal tjantings do. Electric tjantings are also available.

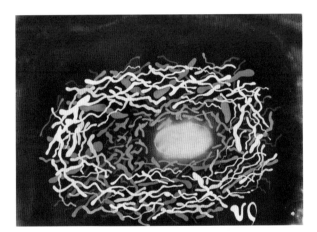

Fabric (Nest Study #1) by Vicki Jensen

testing for correct wax temperature

These steps are identical, whether you are painting, dyeing, or discharging.

1. Stretch and pin fabric to your padded printing surface (see page 10). If the padded surface has a layer of plastic sheeting on it, remove it so the hot wax does not melt the plastic.

2. Put about a pound of wax (a quart container full of wax flakes = 1 pound) into the frying pan, and turn the heat to about 200°–225°. Melt the wax until it is transparent.

3. Test the temperature by putting a metal fork or spatula into the wax, and leaving it there for a minute or so.

4. Remove the spatula, and let the excess wax drip back into the pan. If the wax hardens (turns white) on the implement when you remove it from the pan, put it back, and leave it there for another minute.

5. Immediately stamp the wax onto the fabric.

6. Turn the fabric over. If the wax has penetrated, both the wax and the implement are hot enough to begin stamping.

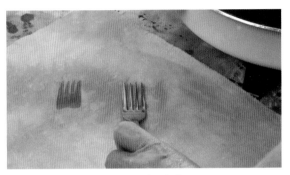

Make sure the wax penetrates the cloth.

two-for-one batik

You can get two for the price of one if you pin down two layers of fabric. If the wax is really hot, it will go through both layers and give you a second imprint. This is more likely to happen if you are using a metal stamp, which retains the heat. Even if you don't get a complete print, you can turn the fabric over and stamp the other side. The two prints won't be exactly the same, but that is a *good* thing. It will give you another layer of surprise. Use commercial or hand-dyed cottons in white, light, or medium tone-on-tones or solids.

Side A: front side of fabric   Side B: reverse side of same fabric

 If you use commercial fabric, be sure you have washed it in hot water and Synthrapol or additive-free detergent first to remove the sizing.

using soy wax with paint

Textile paints and wax can give you quick and interesting results and are a good way to start if you want an alternative to dyes.

Dilute textile paint with a little water or transparent base medium, and spray the fabric with additional water as you apply the paint with a sponge brush. The paint will spread.

Spread paint with a foam brush.

If you are using several colors, apply them and blend them all in the first layer.

Spray with water to spread the paint.

Paint stays on the surface, so adding another layer after the fabric has been ironed and waxed a second time can cause unattractive buildup unless the second layer is very thin.

Darker colors, such as black or dark blue, add drama to the finished piece when you paint them around or over waxed areas.

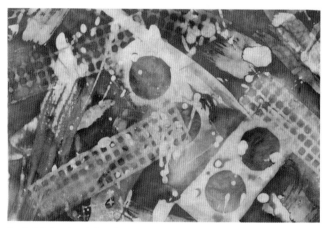

Batik fabric after it has been washed and dried

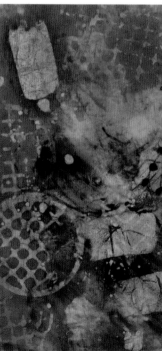

Batiks created with paint, brushwork, and potato masher

You can experiment with out-of-date or ugly fabrics from your stash. (We all have piles of these, don't we?) In most cases, they can only improve.

Before...

...during...

...after

Here is a piece of printed fabric that was somewhat blah.

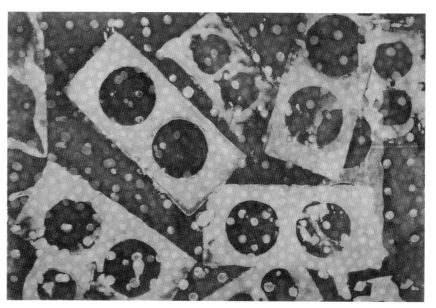
Now, it's much better.

Another plain fabric that needs help.

A layer of soy wax and black paint has added depth and transparency.

IRONING OUT THE WAX

After painting, lay the dry fabric between several layers of newspaper, and iron with a hot, dry iron. The paper will absorb the wax. While soy wax will wash out in hot water and detergent without harming your pipes or washing machine, ironing will give you a double whammy—while you heat set the paint, you can preview what the fabric will look like once the wax is removed.

Newspaper absorbs the wax.

Peeking at the results

To get a crackle effect, scrunch the dry wax, and paint a small amount of pigment or dye concentrate on the area before you iron it.

It is better to wait till the fabric is dry to iron because the colors will be more vivid. But if you're impatient, you can iron while the fabric is damp. Just know that the colors will be more subdued because the paper will absorb some of the wet paint. In either case, the fabric will always be lighter after you have washed and dried it.

using soy wax with dyes

Soy wax and dyes will give you spectacular results for beautiful art cloth, scarves, or cloth for quilts and wearables. You can work on cotton, rayon, or silk without changing the hand of the fabric.

Wax and dye on silk fabric by Vicki Jensen

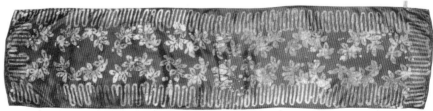

Red Bud Scarf, Judy Carpenter, 13½″ × 56″

Holiday, Rayna Gillman, 28½″ × 33¼″

You can use dye either thickened or in liquid form. Slightly thickened dye is easier to control if you want specific results. If you have thickened dyes already mixed in your studio, you can add some water to thin them and use what you have. Remember, this is art, not science. Whatever you do will be fine—relax and enjoy the process.

Often, I use the dye concentrate (see below), applying the dye with a foam brush and spraying as I go along, to move the dye across the fabric and dilute the concentrated color.

dye concentrate

Reminder: When mixing dyes, wear your dust mask until the dye powder is dissolved in the liquid.

To make 1 cup of dye concentrate, use 1 tablespoon of dye powder. Add enough water or urea water* to make a paste, and then add the rest of a cup of urea water. Halve the recipe for smaller quantities.

If you live in a dry climate, urea can help dye penetrate the fabric. Make urea water by mixing 9 tablespoons of urea with 1 quart of warm water. If you don't use all the dye concentrate and it begins to smell like ammonia, discard the dye concentrate.

DON'T FORGET THE SODA ASH

The fabric must be dry when you stamp the wax, or it will cool on the surface and won't penetrate the cloth. You can presoak some fabric in soda ash solution (page 47), let it dry, and put it away. Apply soy wax to the soda-soaked fabric. When the wax has cooled, spray the waxed fabric with cold water to moisten it just before you paint on the dye: the water will not harm the soy wax and blending will be easier.

 Remember, the more water you spray onto the fabric, the lighter the color will be.

If you don't have presoaked fabric, you can either add soda ash to the dye just before you paint it on or spray soda ash solution on the waxed cloth just before painting the dye on. This is a more spontaneous way to work.

 Start with small amounts of dye because once you have added soda ash, it weakens within a few hours.

soda ash/dye

- To 1 cup dye concentrate, add 1½ teaspoons soda ash dissolved in a little hot water.

- To ½ cup dye concentrate, add ¾ teaspoon soda ash.

- To ¼ cup dye concentrate, add ½ teaspoon soda ash.

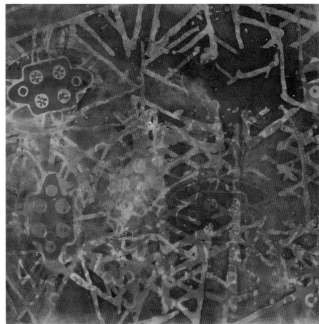

This piece has been waxed again and painted with dye a second time.

With dyes, you can use more than one color in the same layer (as you can with paint). Or, if you want to add more color and complexity to your fabric, you can rewax and dye again. Because dye penetrates the fabric, you will not get the buildup you get with paint, and the fabric will not stiffen with the additional pigment.

using soy wax with discharge

If you are working with discharge, you can use soy wax as a resist and get wonderful results. You can work on previously dyed, commercial, or black PFD fabric. You can buy discharge paste or make your own with Thiox as follows:

recipe: discharge paste

- 1 teaspoon soda ash
- 1 teaspoon Thiox (thiourea dioxide) powder
- ½ cup sodium alginate print paste

Dissolve soda ash in a bit of hot water, add the Thiox powder and print paste, and mix. Thiox paste will keep for several weeks in the refrigerator.

tip   *Be sure you write "Thiox—do not eat!" on the container unless you have a separate fridge for dyes.*

Remember, this is a spontaneous process. The drips and random blobs are part of the work of your hands. If you had wanted perfection, you would not be reading this book! Reminder: Use safety precautions. Wear a respirator, and work outside or in an area with good ventilation.

1. Stamp your fabric with soy wax.

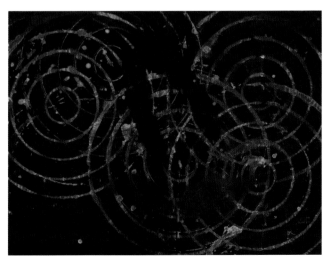

Waxed fabric

2. Lay the fabric on newspaper.

3. Paint on the discharge paste or Thiox paste.

4. Put the fabric between layers of newspaper. Heat and moisture activate discharge paste and Thiox, so a steam iron will remove some of the wax and the color at the same time. Some people prefer steaming the fabric in a pot, but ironing with steam will allow you to control the amount of discharge that takes place. Spray the newspaper with water if you wish to create more steam or use a dry iron.

5. Check frequently to see what is happening to the fabric.

As you see, the waxed areas have remained dark.

Remember, soy wax and Thiox or discharge paste will work. Bleach is not activated by heat and moisture, so it is best not to use bleach with soy wax.

tip   *Thiox and Jacquard Discharge Paste may discharge differently; you may want to experiment with both.*

other ways to use soy wax

ON PAPER

If you make books or do mixed-media collage, you can stamp paper with soy wax, paint it with dye, and iron it.

This mulberry paper took both the wax and dye beautifully.

You can add age or texture to paper with soy wax.

This photo transfer of my great-grandmother's passport onto paper lacked the "old" feeling that I wanted. I dipped it in soy wax and when it dried I scrunched it to create crackle, painted it with a dye solution, and ironed it. Instant age—and an implied story.

Image transfer, wax, and dye on watercolor paper

ON A SCREEN

Earlier in the book (page 32), we used blue glue as a resist on a screen. You can do the same thing with soy wax. Like glue, soy wax is temporary and will wash out when you wash the paint, dye, or discharge agent out of the screen with hot water, detergent, and a sponge. If any wax is left, you can iron the screen between newspaper sheets.

 You may want to keep a screen dedicated to wax resist.

The next time you dip a tjap, stamp, or found object in soy wax, stamp on a silkscreen instead of on the fabric. Wait till the wax dries, then screen onto fabric.

Using soy wax on a screen

If you prefer to put your individual mark on the screen, you need only dip a brush in soy wax and paint random marks on the screen.

Brush soy wax on a screen.

Apply textile paint with a squeegee.

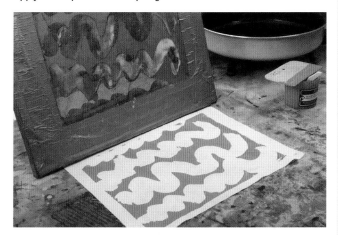

Result: Screened fabric with a unique design

There's no end to what you can do once you start to experiment. Soy wax is safe, easy to use, and versatile. Enjoy it!

rubbings

child's play

Remember crayon rubbings? Many of us did them as children: we put something under a piece of paper, rubbed with a crayon, and a design magically appeared. Easy and fun! Crayon rubbings are still easy and fun, and they are an effective way to add design and texture to fabric in an instant when you don't feel like making a mess with paints or dyes. In fact, sometimes they are the best way to add a finishing touch.

supplies

- Paintstiks
- Fabric crayons
- Oil pastels
- Fabric paints
- Newsprint or paper towels
- Iron
- Textured items (corrugated cardboard, wire grids, etc.)
- Items with raised lettering

Affiches, Rayna Gillman, 39½″ × 31½″

rubbings with dry pigments

Dry pigments include Paintstiks or oil sticks (oil paints in stick form); oil pastels, which are ground pigment in a slight amount of oil and wax; and crayons, which are wax-based. All will work on paper, canvas, cotton, rayon, and silk, and all can be permanently set with heat.

PAINTSTIKS OR OIL STICKS

These are self-drying and will form a skin at the tip. You need to gently peel away the skin before you use them. A little pigment goes a long way, so rub gently at first, until you get the feel of it. It is more effective to rub in one direction.

OIL PASTELS

Sometimes known as pastel dye sticks or fabric crayons, these are widely available in art supply stores. They do not form a skin, and they dry more quickly than oil sticks.

SETTING DRY PIGMENTS

Ironing oil pastels or crayons will make them permanent. Try to let the fabric dry for 24 hours before you iron to heat set; the pigment will be less likely to sink into the fabric and disappear. Iron the fabric between sheets of paper towel or newsprint, moving the paper as you iron. The paper will absorb the oil and set the color. When the pigment no longer makes marks on the paper, it is permanent. You can over-dye and wash and the print will remain.

 In a pinch, you can use regular crayons, although the color will not be as intense.

ADDING TEXTURE

You can add a few quick lines in various places on the fabric by putting a textured object under the fabric and rubbing. Because you are working with a dry medium that is easy to control, you can select the areas you wish to rub without worrying about smearing in other places.

Silver oil stick on gelatin print

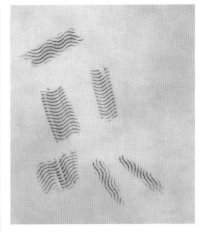

Add random lines for texture.

 Pin fabric tautly to your print board, and slip the item under the fabric. Pinning the fabric will prevent it from moving and smearing while you rub.

A blue oil pastel and a copper oil stick transformed this unevenly dyed fabric.

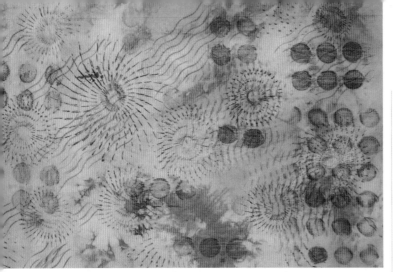

Or, you can create an overall pattern on the cloth. This piece was printed by putting various kitchen implements underneath the pinned fabric and rubbing with oil pastels.

You may be surprised at how versatile familiar household objects are and how varied the results are, depending on how you use the objects. While you can purchase rubbing plates at the art supply store, it's fun to discover your own patterns on items around the house.

This is the bottom of a plastic plate from a supermarket cake.

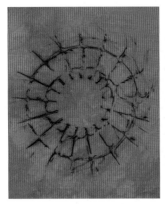 

If you turn it over, you might find another instance of two-for-one printing.

It's just a matter of looking at everything with new eyes and asking yourself "what if?"

ADDING TEXT

Gravestone rubbings are the most familiar sources of rubbed text, but there are lots of other options. Look down as you walk: manhole covers, sewer grates, water line covers, and the like have beautiful raised letters and patterns.

Once, unable to resist "City of Dallas Sewers," I was on my hands and knees doing a rubbing. A truck driver saw me, slammed on his brakes, and got out to ask, "Lady, are you okay?" My answer: "I'm fine. I'm an artist." He rolled his eyes and drove away.

This is a manhole cover from a village in England. Unprepared for such a find, I had to travel to a larger town for fabric crayons and muslin before I could do this rubbing. All those W's were just too wonderful to ignore.

Rubbings are the best way to transfer signs and license plates with raised print because you can pinpoint where you want to rub and easily control the pressure of your hand. In fact, there is no other direct way to transfer the print so it reads in the right direction.

OTHER PATTERNS

If you want to capture the design on that beautiful shell you found, or remember how small your child's sneaker used to be, take out your crayons and rub.

Assorted rubbings

If you are rubbing an item that is not flat, stretch the fabric, and pin around the item so it stays put while you rub.

Don't forget to check the soles of your sneakers, boots, and sandals, which often have wonderful patterns for the taking. If you raid your closets (or local thrift shops), you're likely to create something like the rather whimsical piece of fabric at right.

Shoe rubbings from the Gillman family closets

Rubbings with Paint

There may be times when you have a brayer in hand and want to use up that last bit of paint. This is a method I call reverse stamping. It's like doing a rubbing, but with a brayer and a little bit of paint. Come with me.

1. Spoon about ½ teaspoon of paint onto your palette, and roll it onto the brayer. Use the paint sparingly; this is really a case in which less is more.

2. Slip the item under the pinned fabric, and roll the brayer gently over the fabric until the marks come through.

Apply paint with brayer.

With this method of rubbing you can expect blobs and smudges, but don't worry—additional smudges just add character. Remember, if you want perfection, you can buy it.

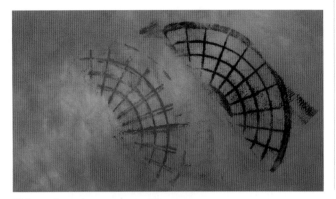

Blobs and smudges are part of the process.

The No Parking sign and my old license plate were transferred with rubbing for this urban quilt. I put them under the fabric and rolled paint carefully (and sparingly) over the raised letters with a brayer.

As usual, I urge you to play. Rubbings, whether with dry pigments or paint and a brayer, make excellent accents and are sometimes just what you need for a finishing touch when you go back into a piece of fabric.

In the next chapter we will look at other ways to go back in and add more layers to cloth.

Affiches, Rayna Gillman, 39½˝ × 31½˝

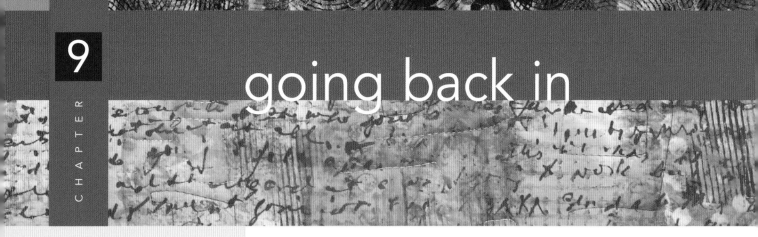

going back in

My studio mate is a painter. Like me, she never considers anything finished in the first round. And like me, she goes back into her work again and again till she has added enough to be able to say, "It's done." While this book is about printing with found objects, it is also about printing in layers.

why go back in?

- **You don't like the color of your fabric.** I began adding layers to my dyed fabric because I was never happy with the way it turned out. Today, when I dye, it is primarily to print on.

- **You've printed and think it's bland.** Maybe it is. But sometimes you just need a bit of blandness. Cut off a smidgen, add something else, and see how you feel about it before you add to the whole piece.

- **Your printed fabric has blobs and misprints.** It's a design opportunity! If you add something else you might not notice what bothers you.

If Not Now, When?, Rayna Gillman, 31½″ × 29″

- **You want related pieces.** Vary the scale. Vary the shapes and keep the colors the same, or vary the colors and keep the shapes related. There are lots of ways to create related fabric.

- **The fabric is just plain ugly.** Cut it into little bits and strips and it will be great!

working in layers

No matter what you print in the first go-round, in most cases it is just a start. You might like it as is; if you do, put it aside and look at it again later to see if it needs something else. If you're not happy with your first effort, don't despair! Remember what we said at the beginning of the book: "If you don't like it, add another layer or two." Not only does layering add complexity and interest to your fabric, it covers a multitude of mistakes. If you don't like the color, add another. If you have an unintended blob of paint, add another couple of blobs somewhere else on the fabric and no one will know it wasn't supposed to be there.

ANATOMY OF A LAYERED PIECE

Adding layers can be intentional and progressive. You may print, see how it looks, and add gradually until you are pleased with the fabric. Or, you might reevaluate a previously printed fabric and decide to go back in.

Let's follow the progression of some stamped fabric to see what happens when we add a few layers.

1. This piece, printed with the bottom of a rubber doorstop, looks rather barren.

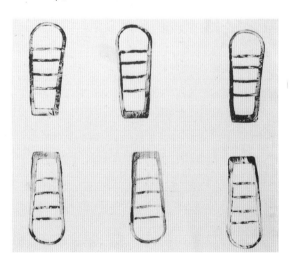

2. Armed with a pool-noodle slice, a sponge roller, some construction fence, and a berry container, I filled in the blank spaces.

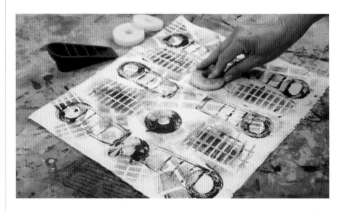

3. To finish the piece I turned to more conventional items: rubber stamps. Found objects are intriguing to use but you don't have to limit yourself. By all means, go through the rubber stamps in your collection, and use them!

4. After I stamped, I sponged on some yellow paint and spritzed the fabric with water to soften the effect. Now it was finished.

tools, methods, and media

There are myriad ways to go back into a piece of fabric and make it even better. You can overlay your first layer by screening, waxing, over-dyeing, stamping, discharging, rubbing, doodling, or any combination you can imagine.

GOING BACK IN WITH A SYRINGE

One of my favorite tools for adding accents with paint or thickened dye is a disposable plastic syringe with a curved tip.

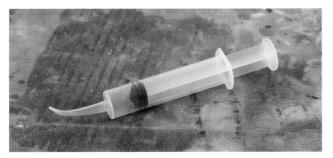

Curved-tip syringe

It may take a bit of practice to feel a sense of control when you write or draw with this tool, but it is worth the effort. You can ask your dentist or veterinarian for one, or do a search for "curved tip syringe" on the Internet. Clean the syringe with water and a thin bamboo skewer.

This fabric already had several layers before text and outlines were added with a syringe.

This piece, screened with newspaper strips, needed some accents.

I used a syringe and added a few dabs of paint with the edge of a credit card, and now the piece has more definition.

 tip *When using a syringe, hold it with the tip on the fabric, not suspended above it. Use minimal pressure. It takes some practice to get the feel of it.*

Sometimes, when you are feeling playful and want to doodle or draw, the syringe can be a toy.

Detail from *Urban Landscape*, quilt on page 45

Other times, it can be just what you need to finish a serious piece of work. *Cacophony* started as a too-bright-for-my-taste yellow hand-dye. I screened with thickened dye, stamped with found objects, and was still not happy. Then I wrote all over the fabric with a syringe and added a strip of hand-stamped fabric. Done!

Cacophony, Rayna Gillman, 23″ × 18″

The handwriting creates contrast and a focal point for Judi Eichler's piece, which has layers of gelatin printing, screening, stamping, and rubbings with dry pigment and paint.

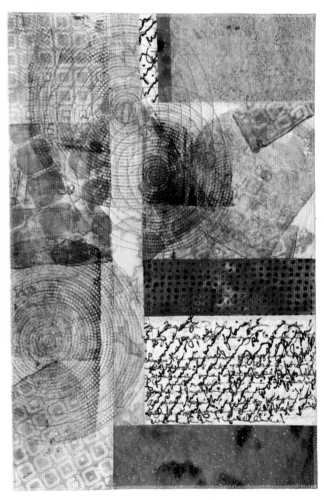

Spinning My Wheels, Judi Eichler, 14″ × 21″

GOING BACK IN WITH THERMOFAX SCREENS

The Thermofax is another favorite tool. Also known as transparency makers, Thermofaxes were made by 3M years ago for cutting stencils and making transparencies before there were copy machines. They are no longer made in the United States, but if you buy a used one, you can cut stencils for screenprinting.

If you don't have access to a machine, there are services that will make screens at a reasonable cost if you send them images from a laser printer or carbon-toner copier. If you Google "thermofax screens," you can find sources on the Internet where you can purchase machines, supplies, and even ready-made screens.

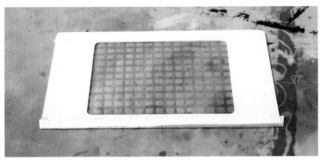

Thermofax screen

Thermofax screens will last through many printings if you treat them gently.

When using a Thermofax screen, use less squeegee pressure than you would use on a regular silkscreen.

This hand-dyed fabric was printed with Thermofax screens. The background fabric was too dark, but when I went back in with discharge paste through the same screens, it made a difference.

If Not Now, When?, Rayna Gillman, 31½˝ × 29˝

GOING BACK IN WITH STAMPS

As you have seen, commercial stamps are handy for adding finishing touches to fabric that just needs *something*.

Mimi Wohlberg overlaid a layer of screened newspaper strip with a text stamp to unify the surface. A bit of glitter paint makes a bright finishing touch to this wholecloth quilt.

To the Point, Mimi Wohlberg, 25½˝ × 22˝

The stamps and stencils Linda Witte Henke used on this gelatin-printed cloth included an empty spool, a game piece, and a faux finishing tool.

River Red, Linda Witte Henke, 24˝ × 24˝

GOING BACK IN WITH THREAD

While this is not a book about stitching, sometimes a hand or machine stitch is perfect for adding another layer.

While someone else might have printed on the fabric, Laura Cater-Woods went back into the cloth and created the next layer with stitching.

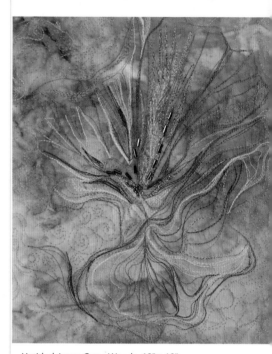

Untitled, Laura Cater-Woods, 12˝ × 12˝,

Many different types of thread can be used to enhance your printed fabric.

can this fabric be saved?

Let's face it: if you've done any surface design at all you probably have some pieces sitting around that you think are just plain hopeless. Before you throw them out or give them away, try some rescue techniques. Most of the time it is worth the effort.

For a few of the reasons listed on page 85, I went back into some of my own pieces to see if I could improve them.

You don't like the color of your fabric.

Personal taste: I dislike pink, and the piece below turned out mostly pink.

First, I gelatin printed with red and purple and washed it out, which left me with some nice background texture.

Next, I brushed soy wax on a screen and printed spontaneously with darker and warmer colors that made a lively counterpoint to the pink. Much better!

You've printed and think it's bland.

This print was too low-contrast for my taste.

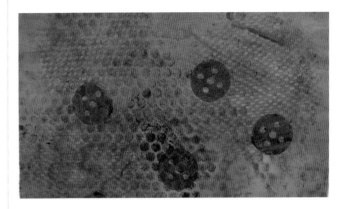

It perked right up when I rubbed it with Paintstiks and the bottom of a takeout container.

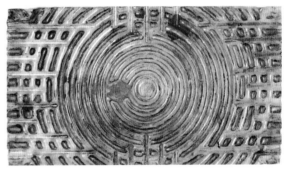

Your printed fabric has blobs and misprints.

One part of this fabric did not screen well and looked blotchy.

I added a layer of text, which adds interest and shows up better on the blotchy spaces than on the printed part.

You want related pieces.

These companion fabrics came from the same dyed piece, which I cut in half. The first one was batiked with soy wax and paint; the second, screenprinted with similar motifs and colors but in a different scale.

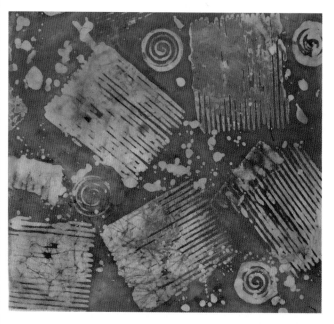

the fabric is just plain ugly

This cloth was a ghastly shade of green. I screenprinted on side A with brown and dark green, which didn't show up. I turned the fabric over, printed randomly, and washed it out. Neither side was good, so I discharged the fabric to yellow. It didn't help.

Finally, I got out my Thermofax screens and printed with black. I suspect both sides will look terrific when I cut them into bits and strips and combine them with other fabrics. There is hope for nearly everything!

Side A: Before

Side B: Before

Side A: After

Side B: After

Good fabric, like fine wine, good perfume, or a superb dish, has complexity that unfolds gradually and takes it beyond the ordinary. But even bad fabric has its uses: it makes the good fabric look even better when you use the two together. Happy printing!

supplies and sources

The paints, dyes and auxiliaries, discharge paste, soy wax, screens, PFD fabrics, and batting recommended in this book are available from the following sources. Check the suppliers' websites for details.

dyes, auxiliaries, discharge paste, soy wax, screens, and other supplies

Pro Chemical & Dye
P.O. Box 14
Somerset, MA 02726
Orders: 800-228-9393 (800-2 BUY DYE)
Customer Service or Technical
    Support: 508-676-3838
www.prochemical.com

Dharma Trading
Orders: 800-542-5227
www.dharmatrading.com

Dick Blick Art Materials
Orders: 800-828-4548
www.dickblick.com

Jack Richeson & Company, Inc.
Manufacturer of Shiva Paintstiks
www.richesonart.com

Jacquard Products
800-442-0455
www.jacquardproducts.com

pfd fabric

Michael Miller Fabrics
118 West 22nd Street
New York, NY 10011
212-704-0774
www.michaelmillerfabrics.com

P&B Textiles
1580 Gilbreth Road
Burlingame, CA 94010
800-351-9087
www.pbtex.com

Robert Kaufman Co., Inc.
129 West 132nd Street
Los Angeles, CA 90061
800-877-2066
www.robertkaufman.com

Testfabrics
415 Delaware Ave.
P.O. Box 3026
West Pittston, PA 18643
570-603-0432
www.testfabrics.com

Timeless Treasures
483 Broadway
New York, NY 10013
212-226-1400
www.ttfabrics.com

batting and thread

Mountain Mist
2551 Crescentville Road
Cincinnati, OH 45241
513-326-3912 or 800-345-7150
Fax: 1-513-326-3911
mountainmist@leggett.com
www.mountainmistlp.com

Superior Threads
800-499-1777
www.superiorthreads.com

For a list of other fine books from C&T Publishing, ask for a free catalog:

C&T Publishing, Inc.
P.O. Box 1456
Lafayette, CA 94549
800-284-1114
Email: ctinfo@ctpub.com
Website: www.ctpub.com

C&T Publishing's professional photography services are now available to the public. Visit us at www.ctmediaservices.com.

For quilting supplies:

Cotton Patch
1025 Brown Ave.
Lafayette, CA 94549
800-835-4418 or
925-283-7883
Email: CottonPa@aol.com
Website: www.quiltusa.com

about the author

Rayna Gillman works in mixed media on fiber, using a variety of surface design, collage, and printmaking techniques to integrate text and images into her work.

She made her first scrap quilt in 1974, when she fell in love with an antique quilt she could not afford. Over the years, she began to print her own fabrics and became intrigued by the textures and design potential of such items as corrugated cardboard, construction fence, and kitchen tools. Today, using found objects from the house, the hardware store, and even the street, she paints, dyes, and discharges, working in layers to add complexity to her highly recognizable fabrics.

Noted for her instinctive sense of color and her improvisational approach to design, she encourages students to work spontaneously, to experiment, and to use the words "what if?" to guide them. She has taught hundreds of students not only to print their own fabrics, but to use them creatively in their quilts.

Rayna was a featured artist on *Simply Quilts*, and has written for *Quilting Arts Magazine*. Her work has been widely published. She was a juror for the national show Art Quilts Lowell and teaches internationally. Her fabric and quilts have been exhibited in museums and galleries around the country and are in private collections in the United States, France, and Belgium. They are on the web at www.studio78.net and www.galleryfxv.com. She invites you to visit her blog at http://studio78notes.blogspot.com. You can reach her at rgillman@studio78.net.

index

Great Titles
from  C&T PUBLISHING

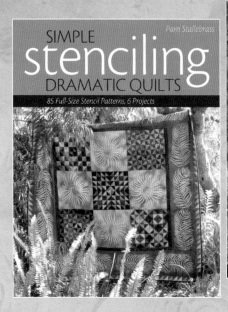
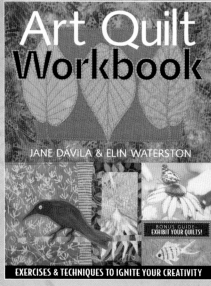
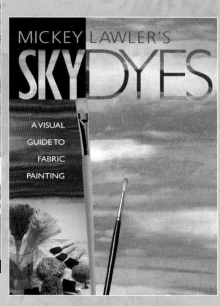
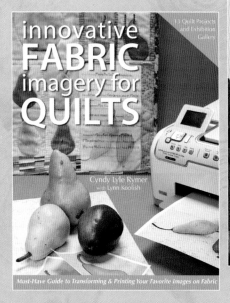
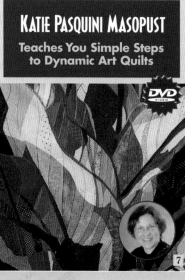